Contents

To Dianne and Red

ART AND DESIGN

A Resource Book for Students

Chris Dunn

Longman

Longman Group UK Limited
Longman House, Burnt Mill, Harlow,
Essex CM20 2JE, England
and Associated Companies throughout the
world.

Published in the United States of
America by Longman Inc., New York.

First published 1989
Fourth impression 1994

Set in 11/14 point Palatino (Linotron)

Produced by Longman Singapore Publishers Pte Ltd
Printed in Singapore
SWT/04

ISBN 0 582 02448 X

British Library Cataloguing in Publication Data
Dunn, Chris
  Art and design: a resource book for students.
  1. Visual arts – For schools   2. Design – For schools
  I. Title
  700

  ISBN 0–582–02448–X

The Publisher's policy is to use paper manufactured from
sustainable forests.

Introduction

This source book for GCSE art and design will provide you with reference material supported by activity-based questions. The questions are linked with work from the past to help establish the continuum between what you do and the work of great artists.

The first part of the book examines the following: drawing, line, shape, form, colour and surface. Under each of these headings, various artists are introduced and their skills examined. In this way you will be working within an historical and cultural context. There are practical study exercises to help you develop your own artistic and design skills and at the end of each topic, you are asked to produce a more extended piece of work.

The second part of the book consists of examples of content. Each topic can be developed as the centre of a network of related studies, both in art and across the curriculum. They can be used on their own or they can be linked in groups, as many of the great topics of art are included here – the seven ages of man, the seasons, traditional concerns of the artist (landscape, self-portrait, still-life, etc.), and opposites such as war and peace, or poverty and wealth. There are many more subject areas which can be grouped together and each topic can be developed further along lines of your own choice.

The book is generously illustrated. I have tried to present as many sources as possible, but inevitably some galleries are better represented than others. Some favourites have been omitted and some minor artists included as, although they might not 'shout' as loudly, they all have something important to say.

Here are a few basic facts to help you find your way around the pictures that appear in this book. You can find out more about them from any good Dictionary or Encyclopaedia of Art. The captions that appear under each picture (where possible) contain:

the title of the work and the date when it was produced (so that you can see if it was early or late in the artist's career);
the name of the artist and the dates of birth and death;

the techniques used (for reproduction often hides the characteristics of the original medium); the size in centimetres (this is important as it helps you to establish the scale of the work); and where the work is located.

Illustrations are second-best; there is no substitute for looking at the real thing and I hope that by reproducing some of the works in smaller galleries I have encouraged you to find out what might be hidden away down the road.

The book ends with information about assessment, a listing of the artists referred to in the text, four pages of 'networks' to show you how different subjects can be supported by various sources and a glossary.

Drawing

The link between the unspoken idea and the completed work.

Drawings are marks, made with a wide variety of tools and organised on a flat surface, usually paper. They can be used by artists to develop ideas into finished works or they can be finished works in their own right. Drawings often give an insight into the way an artist thinks and works. They can show the broad range of ideas an artist may have had in the planning stage of a work. They can also help the artist understand and record details for inclusion in a finished piece.

W. B. Yeats, 1907.
Augustus John (1878–1961).
Pencil, 24.8 × 21.6 cm.
Tate Gallery, London.

The graphite pencil, which can produce fine lines and, as you will see in the task below, can shade in areas of tone, is a tool worth experimenting with. Graphite (lead) pencils are available in many different grades of hardness.

Usual grades are from 4H (hard) to 6B (very soft). This tone square will help you find out the range of tones that is available from each grade of pencil.

Student's pencil drawing.

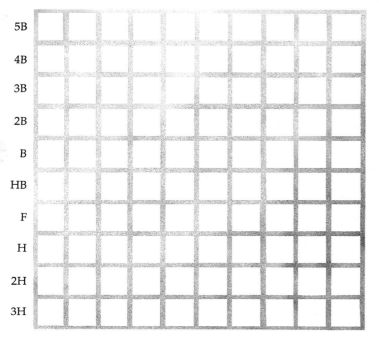

5B
4B
3B
2B
B
HB
F
H
2H
3H

Study

Re-draw the grid above. Collect as many pencil grades as possible. Fill in the squares starting lightly on the left of each line. Make your tones progressively darker until the right-hand square represents the nearest to black your pencil can produce.

A drawing which contains a wide range of tones can create an impression of three dimensional space.

Study

Produce an extended piece of work, based on observation, to examine the use of pencils for drawing. Use tone to create an illusion of three dimensions.

    A portrait,

    A group of interesting objects,

    A garment, folds of cloth,

    A plant, flower or branch with leaves on it.

Find examples of artists' pencil drawings of similar subjects.

Tone can create an impression of space. Artists also use perspective to create illusions of depth in their pictures. Perspective is basically an illusion; it is a system that represents space and the objects that occupy it. The re-discovery of perspective and its development into a sophisticated mathematically-based system was the work of such artists as Pierro della Francesca, who in painting 'The Flagellation' seems as interested in organising perspective as in any religious or political subject.

The Flagellation, *c.*1456.
Piero della Francesca (1420?–1492).
Tempera, 59 × 81.5 cm.
Galleria Nazionale della Marche, Urbino, Italy.

Study

Examine the diagram opposite. It illustrates the perspective system that is most frequently used. It is based on the idea that though parallel lines never actually meet, they appear to converge at an imaginary vanishing point at eye-level on the horizon.

Re-construct the diagram and then develop it into a building or part of a townscape of your own invention.

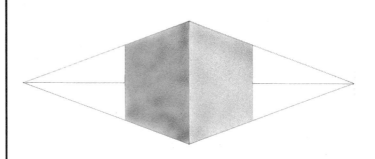

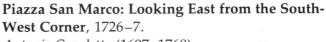

Below is a drawing of three figures from a sketch-book by Antonio Canaletto (1697–1768), a Venetian painter of views. You can see how he has used these figures to animate his perspective drawing of St Mark's Square, Venice. Without the figures the drawing might be considered dull; with them it is full of life and interest. Antonio Canaletto often used a *camera obscura*. Find out all you can about this interesting aid to perspective drawing.

Piazza San Marco: Looking East from the South-West Corner, 1726–7.
Antonio Canaletto (1697–1768).
Pen and ink, 19.1 × 27.9 cm.
Collection HM Queen, Windsor.

Two men seated and a third standing.
Antonio Canaletto (1697–1768).
Pen ink and wash, 9.2 × 13.3 cm.
National Gallery, London.

As artists, when we look at our surroundings we should be able to record what we see. We keep this evidence of our view of the world in a sketch-book. Many artists through the ages have kept such records. Leonardo da Vinci (1452–1519) kept a famous series of notebooks which form a part of the Royal Collection of drawings kept at Windsor Castle. He used many of his sketches at a later date in major paintings. A sketch-book can be a valuable source of material for the future.

A sketch-book is not a 'rough' workbook or a scribbling pad. Drawings in it should be carefully and accurately seen and recorded, otherwise it will lead to errors when you come to use them at a later date. Sometimes it is useful to write notes on a page to help you remember where and when you sketched. This is very useful when you draw from nature where plants, plumage and colours change with the seasons. Leonardo made notes in his famous 'mirror' handwriting. Find out what you can about this; you might like to try it out yourself.

Opposite: **Head and Shoulders of a Woman**, *c.* 1506.
Leonardo da Vinci (1452–1519).
Silverpoint on pink prepared paper, 23.2 × 19.1 cm.
Collection HM Queen, Windsor.

Two studies of men standing, 1730s.
Antonio Canaletto (1697–1768).
Pen and ink, 30.2 × 17.5 cm.
Courtauld Institute, London.

Student's sketches drawn from life.

Study

Choose one of the topics below and make a series of studies of it. Make a page of sketches from life. Draw quickly but accurately. Remember sketches are *not* rough work, but a careful and detailed record of appearances.

Pedestrians crossing,   People on the stairs,
Faces,   Artists at work,
At the bus stop,   Children at play.

Antonio Canaletto painted mainly for the eighteenth-century tourist market. Since most of his customers were English gentry with fond memories of their visits to Venice on the Grand Tour, we are blessed with an exceptional collection of his works in this country. Canaletto visited England and we have some fine examples of his views of London. The Queen alone has over 50 paintings and 140 of his drawings. Almost all the major public collections and many stately homes have examples of his work.

Canaletto's sketchbooks, from which these two drawings are taken, are of considerable interest. He invariably drew figures from life and then 'mined' his sketchbooks later for figures and other details to use in his paintings. He made many detailed drawings of buildings with notes on colours and the uses that the buildings were put to. This enabled him to include not only the grand pageant of city life but also many scenes from everyday life. The shops, shop signs and men at work that give life to his paintings are based on accurate observation, recorded systematically in his sketchbooks.

We are used to viewing the world as a narrow strip at eye-level and the area we can easily see by raising and lowering our head. Our brain often finds out-of-the-ordinary viewpoints hard to manage. Agoraphobia (an abnormal fear of open space), claustrophobia (an abnormal fear of restricted space), and vertigo (a fear of heights) are the names we give to some of these difficulties.

Advertisers often use a dramatic change of viewpoint to give added impact to their work. Can you list and describe examples of where this has been done? Did you find this effective? (You remembered it, so it must have meant something!)

Looking down into the space depicted in the wood engraving by Maurits Escher, it is hard to avoid the feeling of falling inwards. We seem to topple into the picture. Escher's high viewpoint creates a feeling of unease, and it gives a sense of the dramatic to an architectural drawing.

Study

Make a conscious effort to draw from viewpoints not usually adopted. The surprise element in your work will increase its interest and effect.

Set up a group of brightly-coloured objects, and arrange them on a board so that the group can be moved without upsetting the arrangement.

Draw the group, first as a normal still-life at table height; then choose either a high viewpoint with the objects on the ground, or a low viewpoint with the objects supported high above the desk. The latter option can produce very interesting effects when objects are placed on stiff, clear perspex.

Mount your drawings side by side.

Look at buildings above the first floor or shop-sign level. You may be surprised how interesting the buildings are when seen from this angle.

St Peter's, Rome, 1935. *Maurits Escher*, (1898–1972). Wood engraving.

In the picture by Steenwyck (below) symbols of the pointlessness of human achievements are grouped around the symbol of death, the human skull. This type of painting, known as a 'Vanitas' was popular in Holland from the early part of the seventeenth century. The picture is at first glance a simple still-life, a painting of a group of objects. Each object has, however, a symbolic significance. The guttering lamp shows the brevity of life, while the skull points to its inevitable ending. The sword, a rare Japanese blade, is (perhaps) a reference to military glory. The musical instruments stand for life's frivolities, while the books are symbols of human ambitions.

Yet each is handled with skill and a fine eye for detail. The whole picture is well organised with, in its lighting, a flair for the dramatic. Though Hans Holbein's painting of 'The Ambassadors' on page 92 was painted many years before this one, can you comment on what might be seen as the similar intentions of the artists?

Still-life: An Allegory of the Vanities of Human Life.
Harmen Steenwyck (1612–1665).
Oil on wood, 39.2 × 50.7 cm.
National Gallery, London.

If we can escape from the limited idea of a work of art as imprisoned in a frame, then the exciting ideas of Richard Long's 'Hundred Mile Walk' (Tate Gallery, London) become in a sense as real a record of landscape as John Constable's 'Dedham Vale'. Perhaps Christo's 'Valley Curtain' is in its own way as valid a re-formation of landscape as Capability Brown's landscaped gardens. (Brown was a celebrated eighteenth-century garden planner.)

The use of the pen in European Art dates from at least as early as the great monastic illuminators of the Middle Ages. The great draughtsmen of the Renaissance developed the techniques; quill pens, cut from the feathers of geese, swans or other large birds, were the most popular tools. Reed pens, though not as flexible, were also widely used; the characteristic short strokes and hard lines limited the use of this type of pen.

It was natural that artists should seek to support their pen lines with a technique that could describe tone. Artists like Rembrandt van Rijn (1606–1669) developed a style of work which used sharp, incisive pen work combined with a free use of wash (diluted ink applied with a brush).

This wash drawing is an example of the freedom that the technique allows. In the hands of the genius Rembrandt, the sleeping girl is described with a few quick and eloquent brush strokes. Japanese and Chinese calligraphers used similar techniques in their writing. Find out what you can about any contacts between Japan and Holland at the time of Rembrandt.

Hendrickje Asleep.
Rembrandt van Rijn (1606–1669).
Bistre and wash, 24.3 × 20.3 cm.
British Museum, London.

Study

Collect a selection of modern pens: felt pens, fibre tips, ball-point pens, markers, etc. Make a series of figure drawings to investigate the different qualities of these pens.

Cut quill and reed pens and either compare them with modern pens or create a series of drawings using them. Be systematic in your comparison. Which do you prefer?

Samuel Palmer (1805–1881) produced during the ten years between 1824 and 1834 a dramatic set of pen and brush drawings. They capture a magical time, often providing a setting for Christian themes, in the pastoral landscape of the Shoreham Valley in Kent.

The Flock and the Star, *c.*1831/32.
Samuel Palmer (1805–1881).
Brush, indian ink with brown penwork,
14.9 × 17.7 cm.
Ashmolean Museum, Oxford.

Study

A pen, being a pointed instrument, is not really suited to describe light and shade. Artists therefore developed a system of marks (known as cross-hatching) with a pen to enable them to show tone and texture.

stipple   dashes   cross-hatching   scribble

Set up a group of soft objects or pieces of cloth. Draw and shade them using a pen of your choice.

Should you ever need to, you can remove blots from your work, but only if you are quick. Carefully using the corner of a sheet of blotting paper, soak up the blot. Wash the paper clean using water and a fine brush. Use a soft rubber to remove the rest of the blot when the paper is dry. Repair the paper with white gouache, or 'liquid paper'.

The Great Turf.
Albrecht Dürer (1471–1528).
Watercolour. Albertina, Vienna.

Project work

Choose a series of individual plants, or a naturally occurring group of plants, to study. Make drawings, experimenting with different techniques. Produce an extended piece of work based on your studies of plants.

Many artists feel they have a special relationship with the natural world. This is perhaps especially true in Britain, where the tradition of landscape painting is very strong. We are a nation of keen gardeners and plant collectors. Some of the most interesting work of the seventeenth and eighteenth centuries is in the series of illustrated books produced to record the great voyages of exploration and the great botanical expeditions. Even Captain Cook travelled with artists to record the wonders of his journeys.

Fir Trees on Hampstead Heath.
John Constable (1776–1837).
Victoria and Albert Museum, London.

Student's study of plants.

John Constable (1776–1837) was one of Britain's great landscape painters. Probably the most popular reproduction of any picture is that of his painting, 'The Haywain'. He believed in very thorough preparation for his work. 'The Haywain', for example, was preceded by full-size oil sketches and by numerous drawings. Constable even made a famous series of cloud studies so that his skies could be as true to life as possible. 'The Haywain' is now in the National Gallery in London.

In this book you will often find the idea of an extended piece of work suggested. Not all work has to be approached in a systematic, carefully constructed way. Preliminary studies are not always essential but they are a useful way to learn all you can about your subject before you attempt to record it. Opposite is an outline of an approach which might help you answer the question. It shows the relationship between the preparation stages of a piece of work and the finished piece.

	What to do and how to do it! The work process explained
AIM	AIM – You must decide what you want to achieve, and set your own detailed tasks within the subject offered. It often helps to write out what you intend to do (a statement of intent).
RESEARCH	RESEARCH – Look around you and collect, in the form of drawings or photographs, all the things you think you might need. Draw from observation as much as you can. Even imaginative work is more effective based on reality.
REFINE	REFINE – On the basis of your research take a closer look at your aim; now is your chance to re-define it.
COMPOSITION	COMPOSITION – Arrange all the elements you feel you need in your work in a way that you feel fits together.
FINISHED WORK	FINISHED WORK – Complete and present your work. You must then assess whether or not you have achieved your aim!

You may feel this is a very cold-blooded way to approach your work. It is not needed in every case, but when inspiration fails it is useful to have a system to fall back on!

Line

Lines may vary in thickness and weight; this can depend on the pressure you apply when drawing them. Drawings frequently need variety in the way lines are applied; it is this that gives drawings their quality. Artists can use the effects of repeated lines of similar or contrasting thickness to create optically confusing effects. The work of the artist Bridget Riley (b. 1931) illustrates this. Can you find some examples of her work?

A maze can be an example of this: the regularity of lines confuse the eye, giving it no point of easy reference, so that it gets lost.

Study

Design a complicated maze to fit on the surface of a cube. Draw the net of the cube, draw your design on it, and then assemble it. If you can keep your lines of even thickness, then your maze will work well.

or

Use a ready-made, three-dimensional form as the base for your maze. Clean labels off plastic containers or carefully turn cardboard boxes inside out. Find a suitable form and create a maze design of your own.

A freezer marker is a useful pen for marking plastic.

Early mazes date back to the Minoan civilization in Crete. The largest modern maze is the Arkville Maze in the United States. At the centre of this you would find the sculpture by Michael Ayrton (1921–1975) of the half-man, half-bull creature, the Minotaur of Greek myth. Can you find out about the legend of Theseus and the Minotaur? The survival of this story is a testament to our fascination with mythology. A copy of this sculpture can be seen in Postman's Park, London.

Mazes in this country are often linked with the name Troy, as in Troy Town or Troy Farm, both the sites of vanished mazes. Mazes were later taken over by Christian monasteries whose traditional cross symbol was superimposed on the original labyrinth. The monks walked around them in quiet contemplation or progressed around them on their knees, in penance.

Famous hedge mazes like the one at Hampton Court Palace, near London, were a development of the formal garden. In recent years the maze has made a comeback with the owners of stately homes building or planting them as a tourist attraction.

An example of a student's cube maze.

Labyrinth, 1970.
Bartolommeo dos Santos.
Aquatint.
Victoria and Albert Museum, London.

Lines can be subtracted from as well as added to.

Play on Water, 1935.
Paul Klee (1879–1940).

Rubbers can be hard or soft. Soft erasers are useful for cleaning paper around your drawings. Harder rubbers can be cut into slivers for fine work and cleaning up the edges of your work. Eraser pencils can be sharpened and used for highlights. Kneadable putty rubbers can be pinched into shape for awkward corners, though they get dirty quickly and must then be discarded.

Study

Draw a pattern of lines either freehand or with a ruler across a sheet of paper. Draw your lines fairly close together. Create a picture using only a thin sliver of hard rubber or an eraser pencil.

or

Draw a regular fine grid or pattern of lines with a ruler. With opaque white paint or white gouache, create a feeling of 'chaos' by blocking out areas of your pattern. You may need to do some experiments with white first.

Study

Draw, from life, a potted plant or a branch with leaves on it. Make your drawing as accurate as you can. Then, reduce all the curved lines to angles. From your new drawing it might be possible to construct a part of your plant, using materials like balsa wood, straws or wire.

or

Draw a self portrait (again, it must be from life); and then reduce all the curved lines to straight lines and angles.

or

Produce a design based on the contrast between curved and angular lines. Remember, they can vary in thickness and weight.

Botanical Gardens, Section of Ray-Leaved Plants, 1926.
Paul Klee (1879–1940).

Reclining Woman – Dressed, *c.*1911.
Egon Schiele (1890–1918).
Pencil and watercolour, 31 × 44.7 cm.

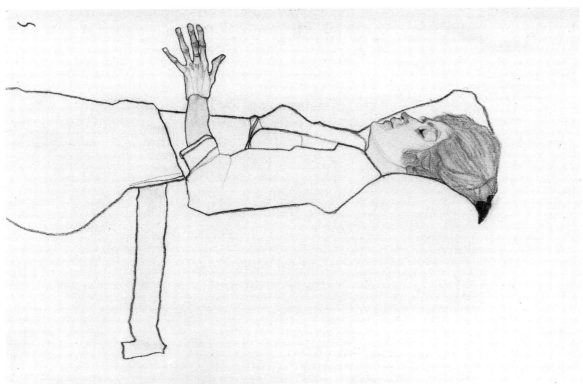

Lines can be used repeatedly to form patterns.

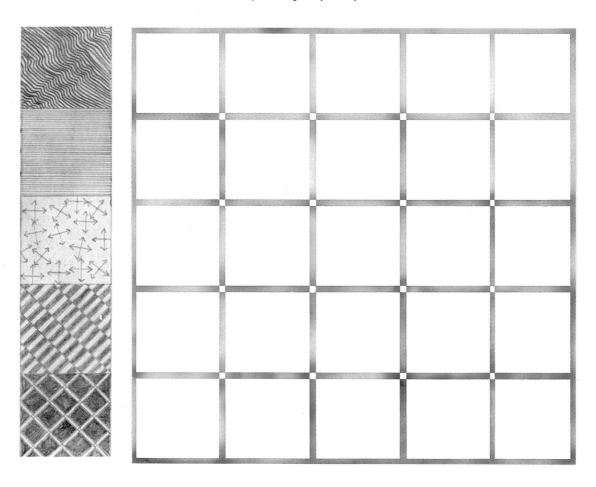

You can use lines to create a wide variety of pattern and texture. Repeating the same simple movements of the pencil, cover a surface (or a part of it) with pattern or representation of texture. Experiment and see if you can fill a grid like the one above with different patterns of lines. Experiment with as wide a range of materials as possible.

This portrait of the 2nd Earl of Rochester illustrates the quality of textures that can be produced by the skilful use of line. The texture of the lace and silks of the costume contrasts with the texture of the wig and the careful drawing of the face. David Loggan (1634/5–1692) was one of the first artists to specialise in miniature portraits drawn in black lead – a technique suited in its precision to his training as an engraver. The art of the limner or miniature painter was one in which British artists of the sixteenth and seventeenth centuries specialised.

Portrait with a Lace Collar.
David Loggan (1634/5–1692).
Black lead with brown work, 13.6 × 11.6 cm.
British Museum, London.

Two Studies of a Spaniel.
Abraham Hondius (1625/30–1691).
Black chalk, 19.6 × 33.5 cm.
British Museum, London.

'Economy of line' is an expression used to convey the idea of a few lines doing a lot of work. They can create an impression of a whole drawing – simple, yet complete. The drawing above is an example of economy of line.

Study

Collect samples of contrasting cloth. Look for differences in pattern, weave and knit. Make an arrangement, and with a fine pointed implement, make a record of what you see.
or
By plaiting or knotting string, silks or wool, create an attractive length of cord. Draw this with a fine pointed implement (hard grade pencil, fibre tip pen, fine line Biro, etc).

Study

Pets, farm animals or wild birds are challenging subjects, as none of these creatures will stay still long enough for elaborate treatment.

Find an animal to draw, either in the studio or in the field. Gerbils, rabbits or the school's pet mice will do. Make a page of sketches. Since your subject will frequently move, you will have to work fast and make every line count.

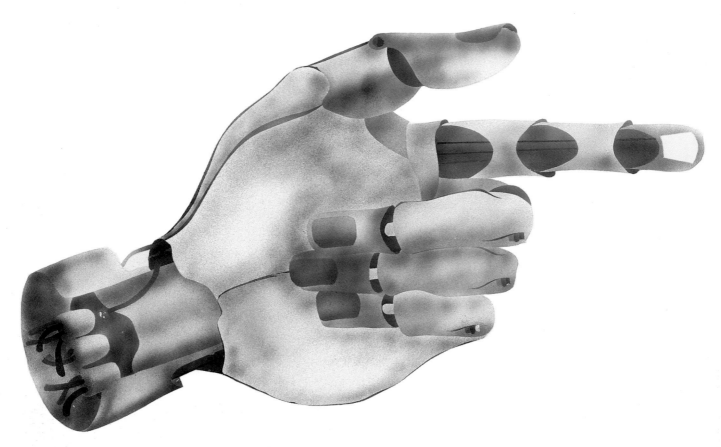

Every mechanical object is preceded by sets of drawings. Almost all the information necessary to manufacture it is contained in such drawings. To give information of this quality they need to be drawn with care and with accuracy. It would be impossible to make a complex machine from sketches. These drawings need to be drawn to scale and to be accurate enough to take measurements from. This is often the work of a draughtsperson. Maps and diagrams have to be drawn with similar care.

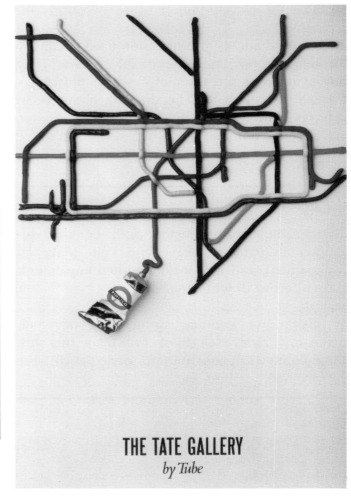

THE TATE GALLERY
by Tube

Study

Design a map of your school or neighbourhood. Try to make it as accurate as possible, as well as interesting to look at. This poster gives information on the Underground routes to the Tate Gallery in London. It uses the very successful London Underground map in a clever way to reflect on the destination. It presents its information in a way that would appeal to and be readily understood by visitors to a major art gallery.

Find a copy of the London Underground Map.

The Tate Gallery by Tube, 1987.
Poster. Fine White Line Design for London Underground Limited.

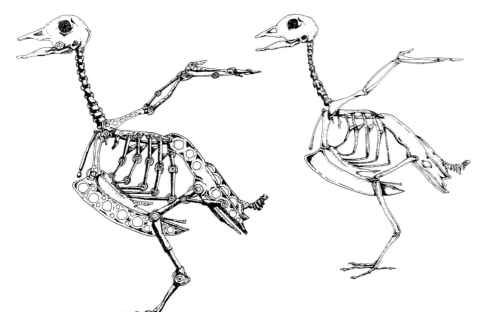

Student's study of a bird.

Three Figures and a Portrait, 1975.
Francis Bacon (b. 1909).
Oil on canvas, 198.1 × 143.3 cm.
Tate Gallery, London.

Study

The accurate drawing of machinery is an important skill, a skill which can be gained only by practice. Produce a series of drawings, leading to an extended piece of work based on one of the following:
The engine compartment of a truck or car;
Mechanical scrap (a visit to a scrap-yard might help you here);
Printed circuits, circuit boards or the insides of some electronic device.

Study

Imagine you are a mechanical rather than a biological creature and draw an explanation of your mechanical insides, all or part of you. You could present your work as a page from a maintainance manual.
or
Make some studies of the bone structures of an animal or bird – a post-Sunday dinner chicken may help you. Develop some studies to produce a mechanised version of this creature.

Francis Bacon (b. 1909) is a painter of our time. His pictures are often violent, the product of a tortured process of painting. Bacon sees the agony in his paintings not as a comment on the human condition, but as a result of the technical difficulties of painting appearances as he perceives them.

He has used medical textbooks to help him in his work. One of them – on diseases of the mouth – has helped him evolve his screaming images.

You could look at similar resource material and see how technical illustration can be used to support artistic insight.

The most usual use of line is positive, that is to say, drawing dark on a light-coloured paper. It is also possible to reverse this process, leaving lines by filling in the spaces on either side.

Two techniques show this latter way of working in a creative way: scraperboard or scraperfoil; and wood engraving.

Scraperboard is a thin layer of card coated with white china clay or silver foil. This is covered with a thin layer of black indian ink. Designs are drawn by scratching away the top coat of ink to show the white underneath, effectively drawing white on black.

Wood engraving is, as you can see from the illustrations, a technique which achieves a similar effect. The illustration above is by Thomas Bewick, from his book *A History of British Birds*. It has been enlarged so that you can see how it was engraved. Bewick was a master of this technique; he was famous for his use of 'white line', in which the image is a system of lines cut into the printing block. As it is the surface of the block that prints, the cut, or drawn, lines remain unprinted.

Study

Bewick illustrated his book with little pictures. He called them 'tale-pieces' for they could be found at the end of each chapter, and they told a story. Many of these concerned nature: trees, rocks, and especially streams.

Draw from life, a detailed sketch of one of the following:
a piece of turf; a hollow stump or the roots of a tree; a stile or bridge; a gate or view down a path; a forgotten corner where the weeds grow; plants growing on a building; a corner of the yard.

The Mute Swan.
Thomas Bewick (1753–1828).
Engraving from *A History of British Birds*.

Wood engraving succeeded copper and steel engraving as the most common form of book illustration before the introduction of photography. It was particularly suitable because it prints from a raised surface in the same way as moveable type. This means that the block could be printed at the same time as the text. This was not the case with other forms of illustration like engraving or etching. Why not? See if you can discover why these two processes differ from wood engraving?

Wood engraving requires a harder type of wood because of the pressure it is subjected to in the printing process. Boxwood is used and as it comes from a small tree, the blocks are often very small. The other limitation to the size of the block is that the engraver uses the 'end' grain of the wood – again, for its durability, but also to achieve finer detail. This explains the small size of Bewick's work.

Many of the early magazines and newspapers were illustrated with this technique. Illustrations were brought into the studio and the blocks cut into sections to be engraved by craftsmen. The blocks were then joined up again for printing. Engraving a block is very hard work and requires endurance, patience and skill.

Since only black and white appear in any piece of work, the illusion of grey can only be created by the frequency or width of the white lines. This is a similar process to the way tone can be produced on scraperboard or scraperfoil.

The Greenhouse: Cyclamen and Tomatoes, 1935.
Eric Ravilious (1903–1942).
Pencil and watercolour, 47 × 59.5 cm.
Tate Gallery, London.

If you are unsure of how to approach the project,
refer back to page 17 for help.

Project work

Produce an extended piece of work based on your
environment. Your work, including preliminary
studies, should be developed from observation,
the accurate recording of what you see. You should
present your work mounted, with at least one
mount of preliminary studies and a finished piece.

Winter Stream.
Michael Ayrton (1921–1975).
Oil on canvas, 57.2 × 83.2 cm.
Aberdeen Art Gallery and Museum.

As explained on page 16, the British have a long tradition of love of landscape. In the eighteenth century, country aristocracy reformed and re-constructed the landscapes around their country houses in accordance with what was called 'the Picturesque'. In 1772, William Gilpin wrote a book called *Observations relative chiefly to Picturesque Beauty, made in the year 1772, on several parts of England: particularly the Mountains and Lakes of Cumberland and Westmorland* (the title may give you some clue as to the fascinating contents).

In it he set out rules for appreciating landscape. He set out what was to be admired, from where and how it should be viewed. He also gave in-structions for the media which should be used to portray any particular view. His book was very successful and acted as a guidebook to the many wealthy people who followed his instructions and became some of the first artistic tourists in our landscape.

For those who did not or could not follow William Gilpin, the travels of artists like J. M. W. Turner (1775–1851) and David Cox (1783–1859) were well known from prints of their watercolours and drawings.

Landscape painters like John Constable (1776–1837) lived most of their lives in the countryside they painted. With the coming of the Industrial Age artists tended to live in towns, travelling into the countryside to gather the raw visual material for landscape paintings. These satisfied the ro-mantic memories of the rich middle classes, the new art-buying public. With a few notable excep-tions, for example Joseph Wright of Derby (1734–1797), the industrial landscape remained unrecorded by artists.

Shape

Guitar and Wineglass, 1913.
Pablo Picasso (1881–1973).
Pasted paper and charcoal,
48 × 36.5 cm.
McNay Art Museum, San
Antonio, Texas.

Georges Braque (1882–1963) and Pablo Picasso (1887–1973) worked together in Paris in the early years of this century. Their work accelerated a revolution in painting. Before this, paintings primarily existed as a reproduction of the subject. Braque and Picasso developed a style of work in which the painting was considered by them as unique, an object in its own right. Paintings were not tied to their resemblance to the subject. Their aim was wider, not to reproduce but to record a subject. This led to the introduction of actual materials into their work: pieces of rope, newspapers, chair cane, wood, or even the braid fringe from a curtain. Eventually this developed into a new art form known as collage (from the French word for glueing).

Works of art became not a description of a subject but a series of views, impressions and even jokes. In the painting above, the first three letters of the title of the newspaper *Le Journal* have been used to invite the guitarist to play ('Jou' being the first three letters of the French 'Jouer', to play). The *idea* of the object, with all its associations, becomes more important than its appearance. The group of artists who gathered around Braque and Picasso were known as the Cubists. They opened the door to a very different way of looking at the world. Before their time pure abstract art was impossible, unimaginable; after them, it seemed the logical development.

Study

A group of objects can be arranged to make a formal still-life group or it can exist as an informal arrangement waiting to be discovered by the artist. Examine for yourself some naturally occurring group, and try to see why it caught your eye.

Make a series of records of these groups. Draw carefully, record all that you feel you need to describe, and explain the relationship within these groups.

Study

Set up a group of brightly-coloured objects. Choose three different viewpoints around your still-life group. Draw the group from each point in turn, drawing each view on top of the previous one. Choose from the lines and shapes you have produced, those which create an interesting impression of the group. Develop your drawing into a picture which explains more about the group than a simple, descriptive still-life.

Study

Arrange a group of brightly-coloured tins and packages (raid the larder!). Create a picture which combines actual samples, labels, colours, etc., with an exploration of shape. This is a still-life, the name we give to a pre-arranged group of objects to be drawn or painted or the pictures that derive from them.

Clarinet and a Bottle of Rum on a Mantlepiece, 1911.
Georges Braque (1882–1963).
Oil on canvas.
Tate Gallery, London.

To show space in their pictures the Cubists abandoned the traditional idea of perspective. Space was created by amalgamating many different views of the subject in a single image, on a two-dimensional surface, rather as the second study box above asks you to do.

Many early Cubist pictures were painted in tones of one colour rather than a full range of colours. Other artists thought of as Cubist, like Juan Gris (1887–1927) who used a full range of colour, somehow produced work which looks garish compared with the sombre style of early Braque or Picasso.

Dutch painters collected favourite or rare items valued by the person or group commissioning a picture. They liked to include pattern and textures, often in the form of richly embroidered fabrics, in their pictures to show off their versatility. Willem Kalf's (1619–1693) painting 'Still-life with the Drinking Horn of the St Sebastian Archer's Guild' in the National Gallery, London, is an example of this.

French still-life painting consisted mainly of objects that could be found in the artist's studio, objects that were to hand. No still-life seemed complete without a musical instrument or an empty wine bottle or glass.

Why do we scratch around the art room to find similar objects, out of their cultural context? The still-life paintings of John Bratby (b. 1928) are perhaps a better example for us to follow.

The Cycle of Nature, 1955/6.
Ceri Richards (1903–1971).
Oil on canvas, 152 × 152 cm.
Tate Gallery, London.

Some artists are concerned with shapes from the natural world, the shapes of growing things. Artists have been absorbed by these for centuries but they found fresh expression with the freedom provided by the Cubist idea of the painting as an object sufficient in itself. Freed from the need to compare the picture with the objects they represent, artists like Ceri Richards (1903–1971) and Graham Sutherland (1903–1980) were able to develop their own vision. Both artists have strong connections with Wales, drawing their inspiration from Welsh landscape and literature.

Ceri Richards often based his work on his reaction to the music of Debussy or the poetry of Dylan Thomas. His concentration on organic shape and form, as can be seen in the 'Cycle of Nature' series of paintings, created a distinctive style.

Study

Choose a piece of instrumental music – modern, pop or classical – as a source for your work. Paint or draw with the music. Let the lines and shapes you make reflect the rhythm and the strength of the sounds you hear. Try to get beyond the visual images presented by the record sleeve or an illustration of any words.

Study

Examine the poetry of Dylan Thomas. You will find it rich in visual ideas. Interpret a poem or even a section of a poem that appeals to you. His intelligent, almost gymnastic use of words, and the contrasts and allusions he uses, could help you create your own visual language.

Look at the delicate work of David Jones (1895–1974) poet and painter, another artist with his roots in Welsh culture.

Red Landscape, 1942.
Graham Sutherland (1903–1980).
Oil on canvas, 68 × 99.8 cm.
Southampton Art Gallery.

Graham Sutherland looked to the landscape for the source of his inspiration and in particular the landscape of Pembrokeshire (Dyfed). He explored a world of strange roots, stones and insect shapes. In his pictures thorns tug at your vision in the same way as in nature they might have tugged at the artists sleeves. The wind-worn rocks and gnarled roots he found along the beaches and in the hills inhabit his pictures – a language of organic shapes. There is a memorial gallery devoted to his work in Picton Castle near Haverfordwest, Pembrokeshire.

Student's drawing of shells.

Study

Artists like Richards and Sutherland delight in the *objêt trouvé*, found objects, objects that suggest to the artists the sources of their own work.

Collect and draw roots of trees, the tangle of heather and briars, eroded rocks, bones, stones, pieces of wood, dried plants, shells, flotsam and jetsam, and all the sea wrack of the shoreline, thorns, brambles and thistles.

Draw an arrangement of what you have found, concentrating on the shapes between the objects, the negative shapes.

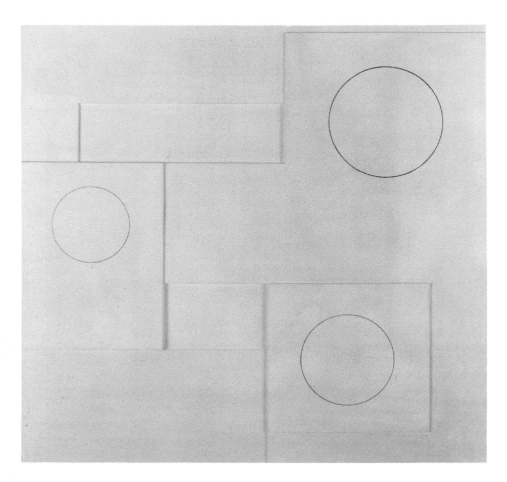

White Relief, 1938.
Ben Nicholson (1894–1982).
Oil on board.
Private collection.

Simple flat shapes, limited colour and low relief are the distinguishing characteristics of the Constructivist group of painters. Ben Nicholson was associated with this group. In the above work, 'White Relief', the only tone is created by the way light falls on the different levels of the low relief surface. His later works show a more varied vocabulary with limited colour, clear lines and well-defined shapes. Find out more about his works.

The Constructivist group experimented with modern materials like aluminium, perspex and wire.

Study

Take two equal-sized rectangles of card. Paint one of them with a flat coat of paint to act as a base. From the second sheet cut simple geometric shapes. Try out different arrangements of the shapes you have cut out.

When you are pleased with the way your design looks, stick the pieces in place. Try to achieve different levels to cast shadows. Experiment with ways of achieving this.

You may use colours but try to keep the colour range simple. When working in low relief you must be precise. You can be sure that any inaccuracy will be immediately noticed! Measure each cut piece carefully and make sure of your angles. Sand and trim any edges; ragged edges detract from the finished work. Be careful with glue; none should appear on finished surfaces.

Study

Find samples of different materials. Often manufacturers have sample books which they send to potential customers. Try to obtain thin sheet metal, metal rods and wire, plastic, perspex and acetate. Since your work will be on a small scale you will not require much.

Experiment with the construction of small relief panels. Each base should measure 10 × 10 cm. This will mean all your work can eventually be combined into one larger panel.

Use the materials edge on as well as in flat sheets. Can you find colours which appear to stand out more than they actually do?

Red Abstract on 5, 1960.
Victor Pasmore (b. 1908).
Oil on board, 76 × 76 cm.
City Art Gallery, Bristol.

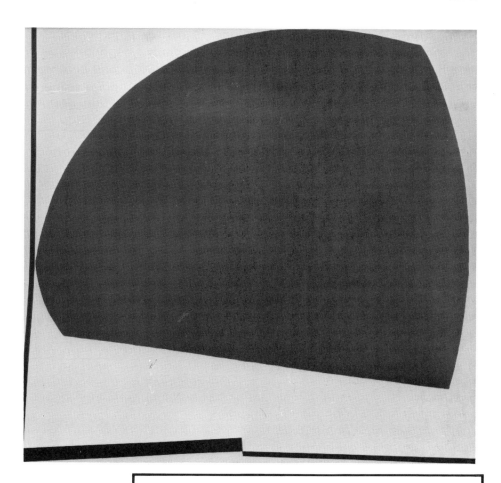

Victor Pasmore has also used low relief in his work, though often deeper than in Nicholson's work. His use of a higher relief allows him to utilise more fully the advantages of the play of light and the changing viewpoint of the spectator.

Study

Make a series of drawings of a simple group of objects, including a diagrammatic plan. Create in low relief a piece of work based on your drawings. If it helps, you might colour each of the objects in its own individual colour.

Use quite thick card. You can increase the depth of your work by using small squares of card to rest each progressive layer on.

Student's work.

Collage (see page 30) is a technique in which materials such as coloured or textured cloth, paper, string, or printed text are stuck to a flat surface. It can be combined with painting or drawing.

Assemblage is a technique for creating three-dimensional work in a similar way.

Photomontage is the technique of creating new pictures and ideas from cutting up and re-assembling photographs. A photocopy of such a montage creates the illusion that it is a real photograph by removing all traces of the joins between the individual parts.

Many artists have used ready-made texture and colour in their work. Some of the earliest were the Cubists. Some artists, as in this work by Peter Blake, have re-used printed pictures. Blake's contribution has been to collect and assemble them on his own painting.

With the increase in good quality coloured printed photographic pictures, the art of photomontage has become more interesting. It is often used in advertising or in illustration. Can you find some examples?

Study

Collect some samples of printed materials associated with your life: food labels, sweet wrappers, tickets, brochures and badges.

Select from what you have collected those materials that are important to you. They might reflect your likes and dislikes. Only you will really know their significance.

Draw a self-portrait and then complete the picture of yourself by making a collage of your selected materials.

Tatooed Lady.
Peter Blake (b. 1932).
Victoria and Albert Museum, London.

A classic use of this technique was in the television programme 'Monty Python's Flying Circus', where photomontage sections were watched and admired by millions.

Use glue thinly. It is more effective that way, and is certainly less messy. Read and follow any instructions on the container, in particular any warnings. Make sure your glue will stick paper or whatever other material you are using. When sticking magazine cut-outs, smooth over your work with a clean sheet of paper. Glue sticks can work very well but they can be wasteful, so if you have your own then do not lend it. Many latex-based glues are bulky when dry, hence the bumps under your pictures. Finally, if in doubt try the adhesive out first.

Study

Choose a selection of daily newspapers for one day. If you are working as a part of a group you should choose different days so that you can compare not only the form but also the content of your work.

Create a collage which reflects the news of the day you have chosen. Since the content of your work is provided for you – even the emphasis of the news is determined by the way newspapers present it – you will have to think hard about the way you arrange it.

Student's work.

This student's work makes comment on what he sees as the inequality surrounding a pay award to nurses. Both the form and the content of the work complement each other.

Holland Park Avenue Study, 1967.
Mark Boyle (b.1935).
Relief/Acrylic, 238.8 × 238.8 × 11.4 cm.
Tate Gallery, London.

Visual signs are simple shapes conveying messages. We live our lives surrounded by signs. The *Highway Code* lists the signs developed to help us find our way safely around a busy motorised world. Motorists only see signs fleetingly, so they have to be clear. We spend a great deal of time in cars; they are very much a familiar part of our everyday lives. Traffic is ruled by conventions governed by signs. They have to be bright colours, simple shapes and pass messages that are easy to understand. The messages they pass have to be the same for all drivers, wherever they come from. Given these facts, it is not surprising that some artists have developed a style of working that uses the conventions we have become used to by reading signs.

In this work by Mark Boyle (b. 1935) the commonplace, everyday piece of road and pavement surface has been elevated to the status of a work of art by drawing our attention to the contrasts in textures and the 'meaning' of the single yellow line.

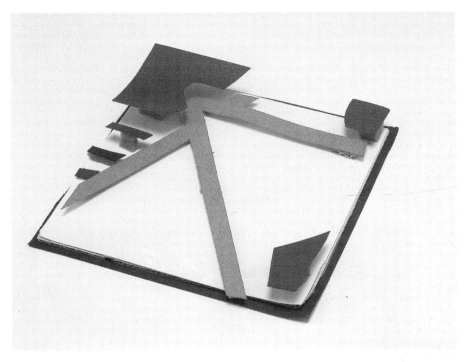

Student's work.

Study

Make a study of road signs as they are in real life, perhaps obscured by plants, overlapping, their meaning confused. Signs seldom appear in the neat, well-organised way the *Highway Code* suggests. Your study could show the real situation.

To obtain the flat opaque surface that you will need, use gouache or poster paints. This type of paint is water-based and dries to a flat, semi-matt finish.

Study

Invent some signs to warn of dangerous animals crossing the road, for example, elephants, lions, or tigers.

or

Change the colours used on a series of simple road signs. See if you can find colour combinations which are more visible or more attractive to look at.

or

Make a collage of overlapping road signs. Enlarge some sections of your collage. Choose one and use it as the basis of a two or three-dimensional piece of work.

Fernand Léger, though connected with the Cubists, developed a very different style of work. The watershed of his work he describes as seeing the sun glint on the cylinder of a 75 mm cannon in the First World War. For a time be became obsessed with painting this dramatically lit cylinder.

Before the First World War, he painted in a very personal style, a more fragmented view of the world influenced by Paul Cézanne (1839–1906), suggesting that nature could be interpreted through the cylinder, sphere and the cone. His discovery of the inspirational qualities of the cannon came to a receptive mind.

Still Life with a Beer Mug, 1921/2.
Fernand Léger (1881–1955).
Oil on canvas, 92.1 × 60 cm.
Tate Gallery, London.

After his wartime experiences he became more interested in working from actual objects and in the decorative use of colour. The painting opposite dates from this time in his life. Léger produced an amazing variety of work during a very active creative life: settings for films, for ballet, costumes, films, murals, mosaics, tapestries and sculpture in ceramics. The list goes on. He played a central role in the development of the art of this century.

A strict regard for simple shapes and for primary colours (red, yellow and blue) can be seen in the work of Bart van der Leck (1876–1958) and the De Stijl group to which he belonged. The geometric shapes of this picture are in direct contrast to the rather free application of the paint. The De Stijl group consisted mainly of Dutch artists, many working in architecture. They sought for purity of colour, working with a very restricted palette, often only primary colours and black.

Piet Mondrian (1872–1944) was a major contributor to this group. Over a considerable span of years he reduced his paintings to pure abstraction in simple rectangles, often on a square canvas. The rectangles are sometimes marked out with black lines and often filled with red, yellow or blue. Through these restrictions he produced work of great power and balance, and somehow peaceful. Mondrian was one of the first artists to discard reference to objects and aspire to pure abstraction.

Still Life with a Wine Bottle, 1922.
Bart van der Leck (1876–1958).
Oil on canvas, 40 × 32 cm.
Rijksmuseum Kroller-Muller, Otterlo, Holland.

Project work

Bright colours and simple shapes characterise the works of these two artists, though their intentions are very different. Make a series of drawings from a sink full of crockery. Make no attempt to arrange it; it is a naturally-occurring group. From your drawings produce a simple composition of bright colours and simple shapes.

or

Flags and bunting are brightly-coloured soft shapes. Fold them so the stripes and other simple shapes are broken up into an abstract pattern. Create an extended piece of work based on your observation of flags and bunting.

41

Form

Lipsticks in Piccadilly Circus, 1966.
Claes Oldenburg (b. 1929).
Tate Gallery, London.

Claes Oldenburg (b. 1929) was one of the artists whose work became part of the Pop Art movement. If one of the purposes of Art is to make us look again at the world we have grown over-familiar with, then Oldenburg's work is very successful.

His soft sculpture, outsize plaster replicas of food, everyday objects produced out of scale and out of context, show the versatility of his vision. An important aspect of his work is its humour. Furniture with impossible perspective, and inflatable food imply a wry smile at our material world.

Oldenburg has prepared some interesting projects on an architectural scale, pieces of sculpture enlarged to a scale that dwarfs the surrounding buildings. Enormous lipsticks for Picadilly Circus, and a vast copper ball that rises and falls with the tide on the River Thames outside the Houses of Parliament, are two of these imaginative schemes. Yet even projects like these, by challenging accepted values, have a useful effect on those who take life, and art, too seriously.

Study

Oldenburg draws our attention to objects by using unusual materials or an unusual scale. Make some studies of clothes on hangers, or folds of cloth. Then represent them in some 'hard' material. Experiment with strips of balsa wood, card, clay or cloth soaked in plaster or filler.

Study

Take a transparent polythene bag and some upholstery foam. Cut and paint the foam to represent brightly coloured sweets. Fill the bag, trying to make your sweets as believable as possible. If you wish, you may sew larger sweets from dyed fabric and use fabric paints or crayons to develop details on your work.

Some research may be required for this project. You may have to draw your sweets before you eat them! It may also help you to save sweet wrappers.

Study

Choose a useful household appliance like an electric iron, vacuum cleaner, toaster or mixer, and make a series of studies from it. Reproduce the appliance you have chosen in an uncharacteristic material. Plan this project carefully. You may have to make a pattern of cut-out cloth or paper.

Scraps of clean white cloth can be joined by stitching or by the use of a fabric glue. These are usually latex-based. Cloth can be dyed by dipping or spraying. Colour can be applied by fabric paints or silk-screen printing ink. Fabric crayons can be used for detail, for lettering or for complex patterns. Experiment! You will be surprised by what you can achieve.

Study

Make some studies of food. Complete the best of these to the highest possible standard. Place your cut-out drawing in front of a landscape photograph. Careful positioning can make the illusion of a very real picture.

Student's work.

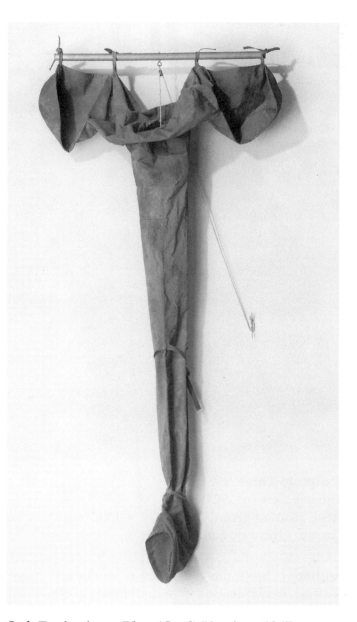

Soft Drainpipe – Blue (Cool) Version, 1967.
Claes Oldenburg (b. 1929).
Tate Gallery, London.

Soft sculpture gives the artist an extra dimension to use. The 'shock' value of common objects altered by a change of texture or by an unexpected softness enables the artist to challenge reality in a new way. Oldenburg's work makes us look again at the everyday, the commonplace. You may not like his work, but few people can remain indifferent when faced by an inflated slice of plastic cake which measures 1.8 × 1.2 metres, a soft typewriter, or sagging bag-like electric light switches. The soft drainpipe on this page is a typical example of a functional object cancelled out by its functionless construction.

Sculpture Three, 1961.
Anthony Caro (b. 1924).
Steel, painted green, 297 × 439 × 139.7 cm.
Kasmin Ltd., London.

Anthony Caro's most distinctive works are large abstract constructions. Welded from steel, often from the construction industry ('I' beams), they are aggressively painted in single colours. This is sculpture that demands to be walked around and to be seen from different angles. His works are at their most impressive when seen out of doors where the lack of a base and uncluttered backgrounds make them seem like odd but beautiful plants.

Study

Collect some stiff card, wood strips and some sheets and rods of plastic. Make a construction that uses these materials in a creative way. Perhaps you could indicate the surroundings that you might choose for your construction. Fix the sections together firmly and then paint with a single colour.

Draw your structure from a series of different views. Imagine that your work is a *maquette* for a much larger piece of work. Draw the completed piece as it might appear in suitable surroundings.

Maquette is a French term for a model; specifically it is a term used when a small sculpture is made as a preparatory study for a larger piece.

Cubi XIX, 1964.
David Smith (1906–1965).
Welded Steel.
Tate Gallery, London.

David Smith was one of the most important American artists of this century. His sculpture, often seen at its best out of doors, is very distinctive: large steel shapes, rough-cut and rusted; geometric and painted (or, in the 'Cubi' series, burnished) cuboid forms jointed at angles and standing tall on a high base. The high base forces the main bulk of the sculpture high above the viewer's head. The works are architectural rather than human in scale.

Smith was, however, very conscious of the human dimension in his work, and throughout his life he regularly drew figures from life.

Study

Collect cardboard boxes, carpet tubes, large sheets of card and any other large-scale materials. Construct a large piece of sculpture from what you have collected.

You can paint the surfaces, leave them plain or even retain some of the printed areas from the boxes if you wish. Since the materials and fixings are anything but permanent you will have to find some way to record what you have created.

This study might make a suitable subject for a co-operative effort by a group of students.

Groups do not need to be of equal size or even work on the project at the same time. They should be based on people who want to work together, to plan and divide up tasks willingly. Success is based on co-operative effort and a naturally-formed group will work together far more successfully because its members want to.

Girl, 1953/4.
Reg Butler (1913–1981).
Bronze, 177.8 × 40.6 × 24.1 cm.
Tate Gallery, London.

The human figure plays a central role in sculpture. From the earliest civilisations to the present day the great masterpieces of sculpture have included the human form. Even in this century when abstraction and the use of new materials have revolutionised art, the human form still holds a central place. Abstract sculpture without obvious reference to human form in its content is dependent upon human scale and human response in a way no other art form is.

Paintings, for example, are often designed to be seen from a single preconceived viewpoint and distance. Sculpture can be walked around. It can be viewed from above, from below and moved around. Its relationship to its setting can be crucially important. Large pieces can be placed in courtyards or on walls of prestigious buildings. As three-dimensional work it often involves the viewer far more successfully than murals, which often form a background to urban clutter.

Study

For this study you will need to work in groups of at least five students. You should take it in turns to act as model for the others in your group. A pose, sitting or standing, should not last more than 15 minutes. You will be able to draw about four poses. Your drawings should be as accurate as possible and, though detail is important, the form of the figure is paramount.

Often the best guide to figure drawing is ourselves. We understand the stresses and strains of a pose if we take up the pose ourselves. We realise the impossibility of an arm or a leg movement if we try and fail to adopt it ourselves. We need to be prepared systematically to check the accuracy of any figure work by direct reference to our own figure and our own experience.

Study

Choose one of your life drawings and complete it. Choose a section from it and enlarge it as a separate piece of work. Concentrate on showing the form.

To choose a section cut out a square or rectangle in a sheet of paper. Move the 'window' around your drawing until you find an area that shows an interesting variety of form. Enlarge only the area you can see through the cut out shape.

The Destroyed City, 1947.
Ossip Zadkine (1890–1967).
Bronze, 6.1 metres high.
Rotterdam.

Study

Figures in moments of great physical stress, like Zadkine's figure for the Rotterdam monument, can take up positions and forms that we might not expect or even believe possible.

Make some drawn studies of figures lifting loads. Remember there is a correct way to lift. If you cannot adopt a position and hold it, then do not ask a model to try.

From your studies, construct a free-standing figure; use any material that you are familiar with or use this as an opportunity to experiment.

On 14 May 1940, after the Dutch had begun to negotiate their surrender to the Germans, Rotterdam was bombed. Fifty-seven bombers attacked the defenceless city. Ninety-seven tons of high explosives fell on the old city. The timber houses caught fire and, fanned by a breeze, the fires burned out of control. Eight hundred and fourteen citizens died in the ruins.

After the war a monument was erected. Zadkine's sculpture, a twisted figure trying impossibly to push back the sky, reflects the idea of the city crushed from the air.

Study

Almost every town and small village has a war memorial. Make a study of those near you.

How successful do you think they are? Do they reflect the glory or the horrors of war? Should they be realistic?

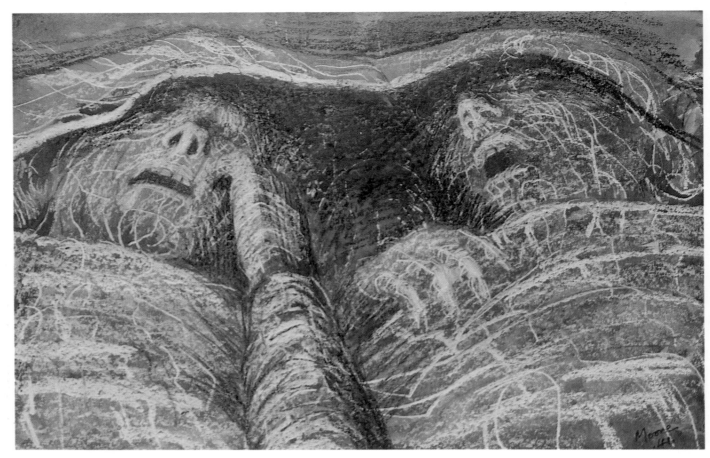

Two Sleepers, 1941.
Henry Moore (1898–1987).
Chalk, wax crayon and watercolour on paper,
31 × 46.5 cm.
Pallant House Gallery, Chichester.

Henry Moore was commissioned by the War Artists Advisory Committee to produce work which reflected the reaction of the people of London to the Blitz. His drawings of people who used the London Underground stations at night as air raid shelters grew out of this work. They are known as the 'Shelter Drawings' or 'The Sleepers'; these are the drawings of shrouded sleepers like those seen above. Seen against the darkness of the tunnels the figures, cocooned in blankets, sleep out the nightly chaos of the bombing. They sleep with the abandon that only the exhausted can manage.

Moore used a very wide variety of techniques in his drawings of this period. In particular his use of wax crayon and watercolours is of interest, for the two media repel each other.

Experiment for yourself with these two materials; in combination they are useful for describing form.

Study

An interesting material to carve into is the type of grey builder's block which, though messy, can be burnished into very satisfactory sculptural form.

Experiment with this material by carving sleeping or crouching forms.

The Tate Gallery, London, has a unrivalled collection of works by Henry Moore. Before he died the artist donated a substantial part of his personal collection to the gallery. On the river bank opposite, and several hundred metres up-river from the entrance to the Tate, is one of Moore's abstract pieces with the impressive backdrop of the Thames.

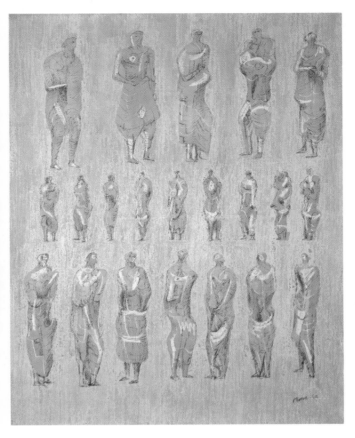

Influenced by Greek, Roman and even pre-Columbian Mexican sculpture (pre-Columbian is the name used to describe civilization in America before its discovery by the Europeans), Henry Moore carried forward the development of the traditions of the human figure in sculpture. The drawings on the left show how Moore developed his forms. His drawings are surprisingly systematic and his techniques quite complex. He developed a method of drawing which enabled him to describe form, going over and over it until he was satisfied with it. Develop a similarly systematic investigatory approach.

Study

Choose a piece of sculpture that you have enjoyed looking at. It need not be by Henry Moore. Make some drawings from it and then try to find a background you think suits it. You can use cut-outs from magazines if you wish, but when you stick your cut-out drawing against it, your final collage must be as convincing as possible.

Ideas for sculpture, 1942.
Henry Moore (1898–1987).
Initial pencil, white wax crayon, yellow crayon, black crayon, watercolour, pen and ink on paper, 50.7 × 40.5 cm.
Thomas Gibson Fine Art, London.

Cliff-tops, mountain sides and the steel and glass canyons of the modern city are the natural home of much of his larger works. The drama and grandeur of the settings do much to enhance the impact of his work. Moore's 'King and Queen' (1952/53) on a hillside at Shawhead in Scotland is an excellent example of this.

Reclining Figure.
Henry Moore (1898–1987).
Bronze.
Tate Gallery, London.

Man pointing, 1947.
Alberto Giacometti (1901–1966).
Bronze, 176.5 × 90.2 × 62.2 cm.
Tate Gallery, London.

Simple figure forms can be made based on a skeleton of wire or even of pipe cleaners. This can be 'clothed' by wrapping it in insulation or masking tape. A further covering of plaster, filler or metal foil can be added. Plaster and filler can then be painted. When making a framework you should bear in mind the weight of covering you expect it to bear.

Study

Using photographs gleaned from magazines create a group of figures in an environment of your own invention. The surroundings you invent should either complement or contrast with the figure types you have found.

Contrasts are often used to good effect by advertisers: city gents in the desert, for example. Can you discover any examples yourself?

Study

Choose a suitable photograph of a figure from a magazine. Square it up or find some other way to enlarge it onto a large sheet of card. Make it as big as you can manage. Paint in the details of face and clothing and then cut your figure out. Create a suitable environment for it.

The pared-down figures of Alberto Giacometti seem to be an isolated exception in the field of twentieth-century figure sculpture. They are in fact another artist's response to the same search for form within the figure that motivated the work of Henry Moore and many other sculptors.

Giacometti thins down the figure, seeking the essential qualities that give it its presence, weight and stance. The figures seem, especially when placed in groups as in the 'Public Square, 1949' sculpture, to be frozen in isolation, unable to relate to each other.

Study

Make a study of figures running, jumping, climbing. Construct, on a framework of florist's wire, figures based on your studies. Create, through the sparseness of your figures, the idea of motion.

Find out about the 'Flying Figure' sculptures of the British sculptor Elizabeth Frink (b. 1930). Can you discover any other examples of other sculptors who have created the illusion of motion from the very solid materials used?

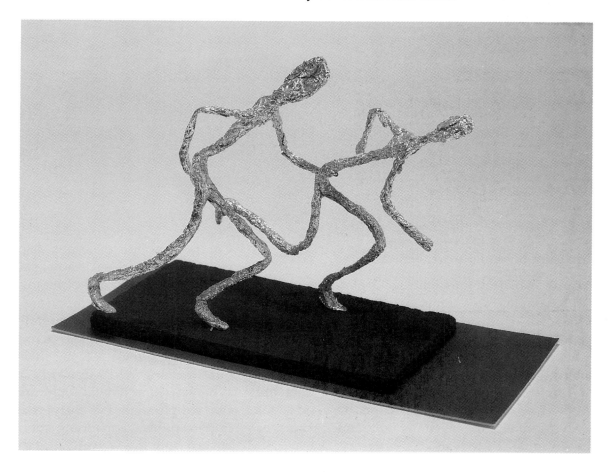

Student's work.

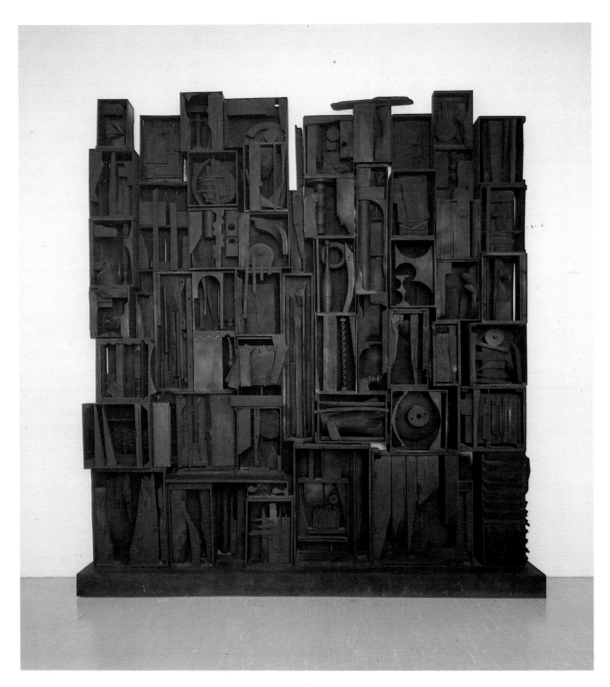

Sky Cathedral, 1958.
Louise Nevelson (b. 1899).
Wood, 343.9 × 305.4 × 45.7 cm.
Museum of Modern Art, New York.

Louise Nevelson's assemblages, of which this is an example, are some of the most dramatic examples of this art form. Groups of boxes are joined together to form panels or whole walls. The objects in the boxes – many of the 'found objects' are offcuts from furniture – are painted in a single bold colour. White, black or gold are favourites. The boxes, tipped on their sides for easy rummaging, seem as full and curious as boxes in an old tool shed.

Contrasting with the static display of Nevelson's walls is the work of the Belgian artist, Pol Bury. The static nature of the photograph cannot do it justice, for the work opposite moves. The balls and cubes seemingly so carefully and neatly positioned on their shelves, actually move. Slowly they creep sideways along their shelves, or without warning jerk upwards against all logic. Whereas some kinetic sculpture moves violently, the sculpture of Pol Bury creeps. Movement is imperceptible, demanding concentration and discovery from the viewer.

Kinetic sculpture uses the power of technology in the service of art. The forces of magnetism, electricity, clockwork or even the breath of wind can be harnessed to create the movements that are at the heart of this art form.

Great painters and sculptors have struggled for centuries to give the appearance, illusion or impression of movement. The advent of abstraction and the work of art valued as itself, rather than what it represents, have brought this form into being. Mechanical artists, always with us, have moved from creating singing birds in cages and musical boxes to making moving sculpture.

In the Tate Gallery, the works of kinetic art buzz, whirr and clatter. The movements are exciting and unpredictable – we are given few logical clues as to what to expect next. As in this work, they have to be unravelled, deciphered.

Study

Find out all you can about the art of assemblage. Study those artists who practice it.

Project work

Make a box or series of boxes which can be joined together. Collect, reproduce or invent a series of three-dimensional objects to place in them. They could be objects that are linked to you personally, reflecting an aspect of your personality or an interest of your own. The objects should be carefully chosen and placed.

16 Balls and 16 Cubes on 7 Shelves, 1966.
Pol Bury (b. 1922).
Wood, 80 × 40 × 20 cm.
Tate Gallery, London.

Student's assemblage.

Colour

The screenprint below is an intricate pattern of lines and curves in a series of different tones. The complicated design does not allow the eye to rest, forcing us to follow its restless lines.

As Is When, 1965. *Edouardo Paolozzi* (b. 1924). Screenprint. Tate Gallery, London.

Primary colours are red, yellow and blue. They cannot be obtained by mixing together other colours. When mixed in various combinations they will produce many other hues.

Secondary colours are orange, green and violet. They can be obtained by mixing pairs of primary colours in equal proportions. Orange can be obtained by mixing red and yellow, green by mixing yellow and blue and violet by mixing red and blue.

By combining complementary colours (red/green, blue/orange or yellow/violet) a coloured grey can be produced. This is more subtle than the flat neutral grey produced by mixing black and white.

The colour relationships are often set out in a device known as the colour wheel. They are best discovered by experiment and by use.

Study

Choose three colours from this list: red, yellow, blue, orange, green, or violet. Make some studies from life of an object or a group of objects. Using your colours in areas of intricate pattern, try and discover how much of your design you can 'lose' without the design becoming entirely unrecognisable.

or

Find or make a three-dimensional object and cover it with areas of intricate pattern in the colours of your choice.

The City of the Circle and the Square.
Edouardo Paolozzi (b. 1924).
Tate Gallery, London.

Roy Lichtenstein was one of the best known artists of the Pop movement. His work fits well into Richard Hamilton's definition of what Pop should be: 'Popular (designed for a mass audience), Transient (short-term solution), Expendable (easily discarded), Low cost, Mass produced, Young (aimed at Youth), Witty, Sexy, Gimmicky, Glamorous, Big Business.'

His style of work adapts the style of the comic book to the subject matter of fine art: the Greek Temple, De Stijl, Picasso or Abstract Expressionist brushstrokes, in addition to parodied themes from comic books on Romance, War or Sports Heroes.

Whaam! 1963. *Roy Lichtenstein* (b. 1923). Acrylic on canvas, 172.7 × 406.4 cm. Tate Gallery, London.

Study

Roy Lichtenstein uses the conventions of the comic book to make his artistic point.

Collect material from coloured comics. Create a comic strip story of your own, and design and illustrate it. It is important to look at the design of the complete page as a unit rather than concentrate exclusively on individual frames.

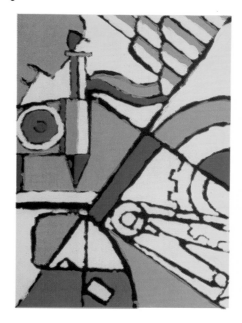
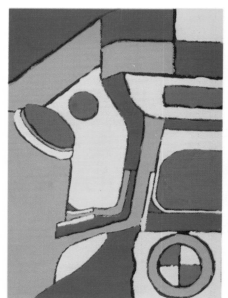

Student studies in colour.

Lichtenstein's work should not be thought of as mere copies from frames from comics. He uses the style of the illustration but composes his pictures with all the care of an artist. He manipulates what might at first seem a restricted style into new and imaginative forms.

His sculpture is both exciting and witty, explosions of dots or ceramics printed over with the dot screen effect of the colour-printed page.

Peace Through Chemistry, 1970.
Roy Lichtenstein (b. 1923).
Lithograph and screenprint, 96.9 × 157.7 cm.
Bradford City Art Gallery.

The title apes the Social Realist work of the official art of the USSR (an art form that supports in an uncritical way the Party view of social issues), but the technique is unashamedly that of the comic book and the brash throw-away products of the Pop culture.

In Lichtenstein's paintings the dots of the printing process are laboriously applied by hand. In neither of the printing processes used to create the picture above are dots part of the process – the dots are purely decorative.

Study

Make a series of still-life studies in colour of the equipment you might expect to find in the Chemistry laboratory. Place the glass tubes, retorts and bottles against sheets of card, each in one of the primary colours. (The cover of this book shows an example.)

or

Make up some slides of coloured gel (the plastic used in stage lighting mounted in 35 mm slide frames is excellent). Make your studies as seen through one of the gels. Be careful to record the way colours are changed by the coloured gel.

Rock Study: Capel Curig – The Oak Bough, 1857.
Alfred William Hunt (1830–1896).
Watercolour, 25.7 × 37.5 cm.
Christopher Newall.

The watercolour above uses only a very limited range of colour. A. W. Hunt developed a way of working from nature in the summer and then producing oil paintings from his studies in the winter months in his studio. To do this his original studies had to be as accurate as possible with complete colour notes.

Study

Make a series of studies of a landscape with which you are familiar. Create a picture which uses only shades of one colour. Since your final picture will be produced in the studio from studies made in the open air you will be working in the same way as A. W. Hunt.

or

Choose a primary and a secondary colour and mix a range of greys which you could assemble into a pattern or design based on a subject of your choice.

South-West Wind, 1932.
Edward Burra (1905–1976).
Gouache on board, 55 × 75.5 cm.
Portsmouth City Museum and Art Gallery.

Edward Burra produced an amazing variety of
work during a long, productive life. From the time
of his youth, when restricted by rheumatic fever,
he developed a fantasy life. Trips to Mexico and to
Harlem, New York, added a touch of the exotic.
The influences of the Spanish Civil War, in which
many European intellectuals were involved, gave
his vision a crueller edge. His paintings often
show the fascinated interest with which he regarded the seamier side of life.

The landscape above dates from a period when
he renewed his interest in the English landscape.
Burra later became an official war artist, peopling
the sands and countyside around his home near
Rye, Sussex, with the strange creatures and
machines of war-time Britain (page 83).

From a study of the picture above, this student
has developed an effective personal style.

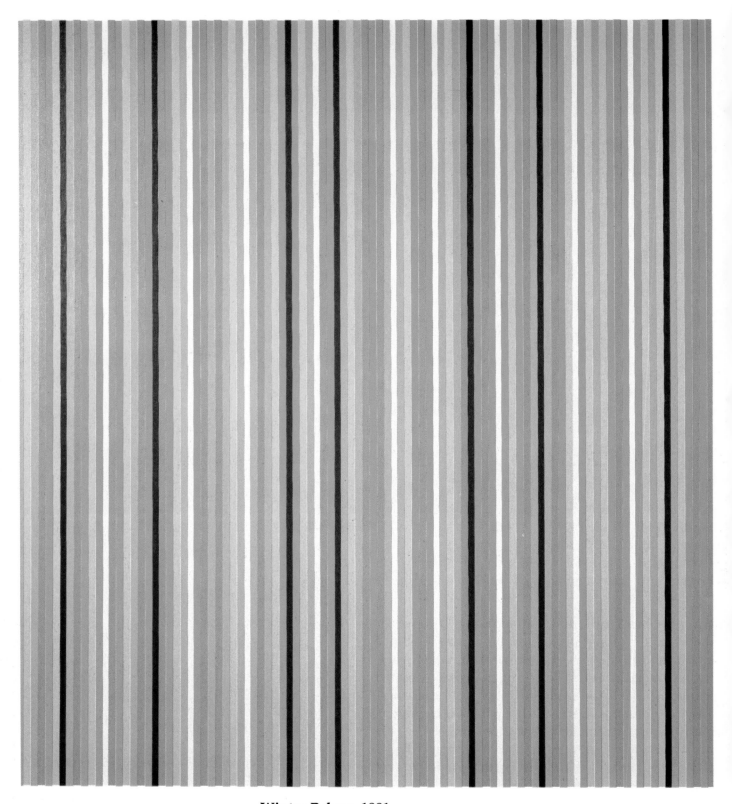

Winter Palace, 1981.
Bridget Riley (b. 1931).
Oil on linen, 212.1 × 83.5 cm.
Mayor Rowan Gallery, London.

Student's work.

Bridget Riley's optical paintings are often so disorientating that they actually hurt the eye. The stripes of colour seem to shimmer; even a close examination fails to disclose the actual number of colours being used. The colours mix and remix optically as you watch.

Using a limited format but an ever-widening palette of colour, her painting style has consistently developed the theme of colour interactions. Compare the black and white stripes of her 1960s paintings with the complicated cross-colour relationships of the 'Winter Palace' opposite. The lack of any point of reference in the paintings gives the eye no focus of attention and so it roams the canvas, driven here and there by the pulse of reacting colours.

Study

Choose a primary colour and a complementary colour. Divide your picture shape into a series of similar small shapes and experiment with creating optical (confusing to the eye) effects. Try dots, triangles or any other repeated regular shapes. Use the information you have gained to create a picture of your own.

Study

Areas of different contrasting colours can create an illusion of space in a picture.

Use areas of colour to create or confuse the space in your picture.

In 1912, Spencer Gore, a leading member of a group of artists known as the Camden Town Group, moved into a house in Letchworth. It was owned by another artist in this group, his friend Harold Gilman (1876–1919). Spencer Gore painted a series of pictures of the landscapes around this house, of which 'The Cinder Path' is one. In these paintings he simplified his subject into a series of broad, brightly-coloured stripes. His subjects were the ordinary, the suburban landscape; it was his treatment of it that was unique. The series includes the bright Fauve colours (see page 65) of the painting opposite – 'Harold Gilman's House, Letchworth'. This painting – now, ironically, seeming staid by the advances in our perception that work like it made possible – was revolutionary in its day. Spencer Gore died of pneumonia in 1914, cutting short an emerging creative talent.

The Cinder Path, 1912.
Spencer Gore (1878–1914).
Oil on canvas, 68.6 × 78.7 cm.
Tate Gallery, London.

Study

Apply a similar systematic approach to a landscape that you know well. You may make studies to get yourself started. Choose a range of colour which you think might give a particular mood to your landscape, for example colours that might convey an impression of peace and tranquillity.

Harold Gilman's House, Letchworth, 1912.
Spencer Gore (1878–1914).
Oil on canvas, 63.5 × 76 cm.
Leicestershire Museum and Art Gallery.

Study

Choose a landscape with buildings that you know well and produce a series of studies in colour.

Apply colour direct without drawing. Aim for a balance of colours and tones rather than a slavish copy of the shapes and colours that you can see. Experiment with mixing colours to achieve harmony in your composition.

Britain was led to the forefront of the Modern Movement by the example of Spencer Gore and the other artists of the Camden Town Group, and the groups that derived from it. The influence of artists like Gauguin (1848–1903), Cézanne (1839–1906) and the young Matisse (1869–1954) helped them to give a particularly English interpretation to the advances of Paris and the new ideas from the Continent.

Spencer Gore's systematic reduction of landscape to simple shapes and bright colours was the result of a combination of these influences with the English love of landscape and his acute observation of its light and form.

Winter Landscape, Cornwall, 1920.
Sir Matthew Smith (1879–1959).
Oil on canvas, 54.2 × 64.6 cm.
The Glyn Vivian Gallery, Swansea.

Project work

Make a series of studies of one of the following
subjects: a derelict part of town, a scrap heap or a
forgotten corner of a farmyard or garden. Create a
piece of work which uses none of the colours you
might expect to find in the real landscape. Your
aim must be to balance the tones in your picture
rather than re-create the real colours.

Sir Matthew Smith, while not officially linked to the loose circle of artists known as the Fauve group, was for a short time a visitor to the studio of Henri Matisse (1869–1954), a central figure in the group. Influenced by Matisse, he adopted a much brighter palette of colours in his work after these visits. His finest landscape paintings were of Cornwall in 1920/21. He travelled to the countryside initially to recover from wounds and shell-shock that he suffered in the First World War. In a state of high nervous tension, he transposed the colours in his Cornish landscapes. In 'Winter Landscape', opposite, the landscape burns with vibrant colours, seen perhaps through a filter of his painful memories.

'Fauve', meaning wild beast, was a term of abuse which, as is often the case, was adopted with pride by the painters it described. It was coined by a newspaper critic in a time when new paintings and exhibitions were reviewed in the press rather like new films are reviewed today.

The so-called Fauves were not a formal organisation, but they represented a group of artists all at a similar stage in their development. Their alleged wildness lay in the brilliance of the colours they adopted and the freedom with which they managed them. Their exploration of the potential of pure colour makes their work appear savage and raw even today.

Fauvism's importance as a movement was its place as a milestone along the road which freed artists from any obligation to imitate outward appearances. The later careers of Henri Matisse, André Derain (1880–1954), Raoul Dufy (1877–1953), and Maurice Vlaminck (1876–1958), show that while Fauvism was not their whole artistic life, it made their later work possible. By not accepting limitations on the use of colour and asserting the primacy of the picture as an object in its own right, their later development shows that the artist as a creator, rather than a recorder, had finally arrived.

The Snail, 1953.
Henri Matisse (1869–1954).
Collage of cut and pasted paper, 286.5 × 287 cm.
Tate Gallery, London.

Surface

On the left is a simple motif developed from a drawing of three seals. The drawings have been changed, or rather adapted, to make a unit which can be repeated to form a pattern. On the opposite page you can see the motif used as a part of a simple repetitive pattern. A motif is a single or repeated design or colour.

Study

Make some study drawings of the following natural objects, making your work as accurate as possible:

Leaves (try to work from a variety of species so that you have some choice);

Vegetables (whole or sliced);

Trees (you can look for the basic shapes that show the different species).

or

Make some study drawings of the following man-made objects, making your work as accurate as possible:

Cogs and springs (the contents of a mechanical watch would be suitable);

Resistors (all the brightly coloured contents of one of the latest electronic marvels);

Sweets (brightly coloured or wrapped).

Choose an effective drawing and from it develop a simple motif.

Does your motif work? The simplest and the most effective way to test your motif as a pattern is to use photocopies, pasted-up as a repeat pattern. Photocopy the paste-up and use white gouache to cover any unwanted lines. If the motif you have designed looks good then you can look for ways to print it.

Repeat patterns can be printed in different combinations of colours. Commercial fabrics from a specialist shop illustrate this well. Any curtain material shop should be able to offer a selection of designs in a variety of colourways. Each different colour requires a different block to print from. The fabric designer has not only to design the fabric but also to ensure that the colour separations are possible.

Student's work.

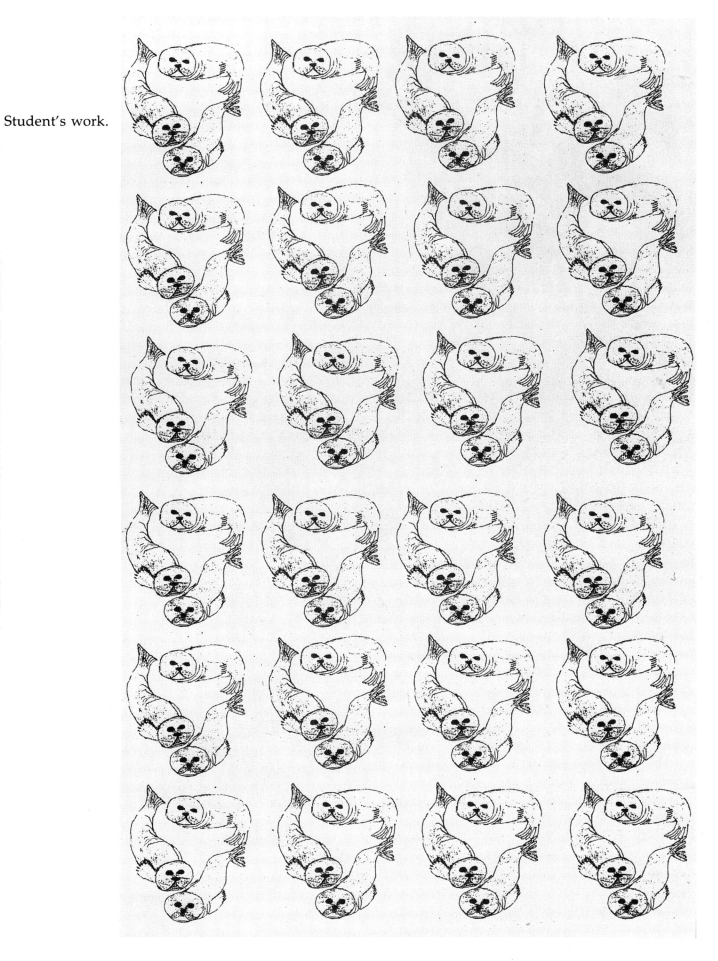

Stylised Cockerel Motif, Pazyryk, Siberia, 4th to 3rd century BC.

Study

Produce a motif based on a series of animal studies. You should draw quickly from life before you simplify your final drawing into a motif.

Your motif should be suitable for a single-colour block print. Print it!

Below is an explanation of the method and the materials you need for printing from a block. Make sure you understand fully what you need before you begin.

Blocks can be made from card, sealed with a waterproof glue. They can be cut from lino or from wood. Their main characteristic is that they print from the raised surface of the block. They provide you with a simple way to print your motif, provided your design is simple; that is, the colours are well separated. Ink is applied to the raised surface. When the inked surface is placed in contact with paper or fabric and pressure is applied, the design is transferred.

To make a simple print using one block, trace from your design the area of the lightest colour and transfer it to your block. Cut it out. Repeat this process for each colour.

Ink up the surface of the block, lightest colour first, with a roller. Press it firmly to the paper. Apply pressure, with a clean roller, to the reverse of the block.

Repeat this process with each block inked with its respective colour. Take care that the colours are registered so that they fit together as they do in your original design.

Some of the most exciting animal motifs come from the fabrics, pots and carvings of the tribal cultures. The process of simplification is often the result of years of distillation, of change related to the complex techniques which many of these supposedly simple cultures evolved to produce their fabrics, pots and carvings.

Weaving, for example, with its images made from coarse threads produces a weft pattern of geometric stitches. A modern design tool which works in a similar way is the computer. Its print-out of dashes is often used in the design of woven patterns. Looms can be operated directly from modern computers – they speak the same logical design language.

Repeat patterns can also be found occurring incidentally: piles of bricks or concrete pipes, stacks of logs, or the pattern of drain covers. It needs an awareness of the world around you, but once you start to look you will find the world full of patterns. Make a list of those you have discovered for yourself and check among your group to see who has the most unusual. Perhaps you should prove what you have found by drawing it.

Stylised Cockerel Motif, Pazyryk, Siberia, 4th to 3rd century BC.

Study

Use the idea of radiating lines or a spiral as the structure to underlie a pattern. Invent a simple motif based on leaf or plant shapes and arrange it in a spiral, or radiating from a central point. This study should show the process from original object to finished work and should be mounted so that the following stages can be seen:
original object – drawing/study – design/motif – finished work.

Study

Make a collection of printed fabrics, wallpaper and wrapping papers that feature repeat patterns. Identify the motif. Perhaps you could re-draw it on a larger scale.

Often, different colourways, combinations of colour, are available. Are there some colours that are used more often than others? List them.

A motif is often complex, repeated so that it combines to give the effect of a larger pattern. Can you find an example of this?

Decoration for the House of Dr Vaquez, 1896.
Edouard Vuillard (1868–1940).
Oil on canvas, 213 × 154 cm.
Musées de la Ville, Paris.

Artists have the opportunity to use actual pattern or texture in the form of collage, for example, in their work; or they can represent pattern. Some interior decorators specialise in painting walls to represent marble.

Edouard Vuillard's paintings (opposite and below) of the inside of a room is a painting of pattern in profusion. It contains so much detail, so much pattern, that the picture loses its depth and becomes a patterned surface. Some techniques are more suitable than others to show pattern or texture. The artist's skill is to know which medium to use.

Study

Construct a grid like the one to the right and with a wide variety of media (for example, pen, felt pen, pencil, biro, oil pastel, pastel, wax crayon) experiment to show a different pattern or texture for each square. Try to match the technique to the pattern or texture that you wish to portray.

These three panels complete the scheme of decoration for the House of Dr Vaquez, 1896.

Study

Make some drawings of familiar furniture: a chair, a television set, a chest of drawers, a bed, or a table.

Cover one of these drawings with a variety of patterns or textures.

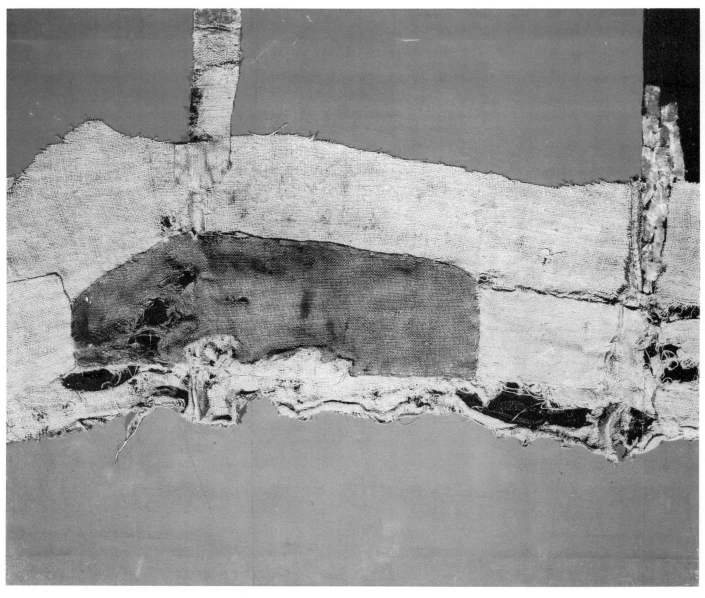

Sacco e Rosso, 1954.
Alberto Burri (b. 1915).
Sacking, glue and plastic paint on canvas,
86 × 100 cm.
Tate Gallery, London.

Artists have often been interested in the surface quality of their pictures. Frequently as we have seen, actual textures are attached to the surfaces of their paintings. Find out about the life and work of the Italian painter Alberto Burri who painted the picture above. Does you knowledge of his life help explain his pictures?

Study

Collect as many actual textures as you can. Try and collect as wide a variety as possible, from shiny foil to the roughest of sackcloth.

Make a panel on which to arrange your texture collection. As your textures may be heavy you will r.eed quite a substantial support. The arrangemer t does not have to be representational. You should aim rather to produce a balance on the picture surface itself. You may use colours on your surfa:e if you wish.

Ochre Gris LXX, 1958.
Antonio Tapies (b. 1923).
Oil, latex and marble dust on canvas,
260 × 194 cm.
Tate Gallery, London.

We tend to accept the texture of paint as it comes out of the tube or tin. Sand, clay, stones or glue can all be used as agents to thicken paint and to change its texture. There are some commercial thickening agents for use with plastic (arcylic) paints. For other types of paint we must search for our own. After all, we are quite prepared to thin paint with water or turpentine, so why not thicken it?

Study

Make some experiments recording the different effects of adding different materials to a selection of paints.

Use the most successful of your experiments to paint a small (20 × 20 cm) panel with a variety of textured paints. Your picture need not be representational but should aim at a balance and harmony in itself.

Relief no 192, 1968.
Sergio Carmargo (b. 1930).
Painted wood relief,
120 × 80 cm.
Gimpel Fils Gallery, London.

Relief no 267, 1970.
Sergio Carmargo (b. 1930).
Painted wood relief,
100 × 100 cm.
Gimpel Fils Gallery, London.

Sergio Carmargo, through the use of a limited motif, in this case the cylinder cut across at different angles and set close together, creates an interesting surface quality. The use of a single colour (usually white) means that variations in tone are created only by the play of light on the surface of the relief. The cylinders may be of different diameters but they are related in a modular series.

Study

Create a relief panel through the repetition of a single simple form. Balsa wood sections of dowel or blocks might be your raw material. The surface you set them on does not have to be flat, and the forms do not have to be cut in a slant as Carmargo does.

Make a record, drawn or photographic, of your work under different lighting conditions.

Inset Wheels.
Michael Rothenstein (b. 1908).
Lino and metal with photolitho insets.
Editions Alecto.

Study

Collect as many rubbings of textured surfaces as possible. Be systematic and record the source of each of your rubbings. Use wax crayon and a thin paper like newsprint.

From your collection create a collage based on the theme of an abstract textured panel to decorate the outside of a public building.

To do this you will have to give some clear indication of the proposed scale of your panel. Choose an existing building, for example, school hall, public library, swimming baths, and make a sketch elevation so that you can visualise your panel in the correct surroundings.

Study

Collect a selection of flat objects with textured surfaces. Print each in turn until you have a 'bank' of textures. Assemble those of your choice and print them in a series of different colour ways.

The idea of monoprint is not new; there are examples of the technique being used in the sixteenth century. Basically it refers to a print from a surface which is itself changed by the printing process and therefore an exact print cannot be repeated. You can use ink rolled onto a sheet of glass (or other smooth rigid surface) as your 'block' and draw patterns or press textures into the ink surface, which can then be transferred onto paper. Place the paper face down on the inked glass sheet and rub gently on the back.

Young Hare, 1502.
Albrecht Dürer (1471–1528).
Watercolour, 25.1 × 22.6 cm.
Albertina, Vienna.

Project work

Produce an extended set of work based on a series of studies of figures in groups. Concentrate on the textures and patterns that are found between the figures.

The texture of the coat of the young hare shows the detail possible with this technique. Dürer used watercolours with a fine stiff brush to help create the effect of fur. Notice the size of the original. Reproductions in books are rarely the size of the original. You need to see the full size to realise the true effects of a technique.

Hammersmith Bridge on Boat Race Day, *c*.1862.
Walter Greaves (1846–1931).
Oil on canvas, 91.4 × 139.7 cm.
Tate Gallery, London.

The startling composition of the painting above shows the effect of a skilfully controlled use of pattern. It also demonstrates that patterns need not be made up of identical units but can be formed from related shapes – shapes that bear a 'family' resemblence.

Student's work.

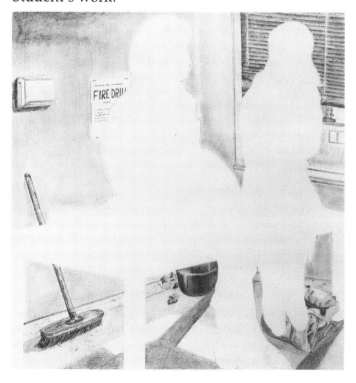

Childhood

Head of a Boy.
Jean-Baptiste Greuze (1725–1805).
Red chalk.
Kunsthalle, Hamburg.

Student's work.

Project work

Childhood is an experience that for better or worse we have all gone through. We all have our own favourite or worst memories.

Produce an extended piece of work, supported by research and preliminary studies, to record your very first memories. How far back can you go? You may have to ask members of your family to help fill in the details and perhaps use some family photographs.

Childhood is a very recent 'invention'. It became possible only after the great nineteenth-century philanthropists freed children from work and introduced a measure of free education. You may or may not appreciate it, but free education was a luxury probably not enjoyed by your great-great-great grandparents nor by the majority of young people in the world today.

What were you doing at the age of ten? A boy in the early nineteenth century could have been standing in front of a regiment of infantry as a drummer, waiting to receive a volley of shot from an advancing enemy.

Find out about the position of children during this period. Perhaps you could design some advertisements for the hard, sometimes fatal work that they endured in the place of childhood as you know it.

In the property-owning classes all over Europe children were considered a dynastic asset. As young as two or three they could be promised in marriage. Often as young as ten they were married and sent to live in foreign lands. No time for childhood for those children who were expected to take their national responsibilities seriously.

In the Third World today children of five or six have started work. The cheap clothing we buy in the West could have been made by these children. Contrast your own childhood with what you can find out about their experiences.

WANTED
DRUMMER BOYS
AGE 10–13
Take the KING'S shilling. Uniform provided. NO experience required. LEAD the KING'S soldiers into battle. Stand in the front of the front rank.
Survivors will be well-rewarded. Those losing a limb or otherwise maimed will be rewarded with a MEDAL from the KING.
GOD SAVE THE KING.

Duc de Montpensier.
Francois Boucher (1703–1770).
Oil on canvas, 89.4 × 70.3 cm.
National Trust, Waddesden Manor.

Landscape

The Falls of Clyde.
J. M. W. Turner (1775–1851).
Watercolour.
Walker Art Gallery, Liverpool.

Opposite: **The Falls of Clyde**.
J. M. W. Turner (1775–1851).
Oil on canvas.
Lady Lever Collection,
Port Sunlight, Cheshire.

The body of Turner's work is so vast; one of the only places to visit that shows anything like the scope of this artist's output is the new Clore extension to the Tate Gallery, London. The arrangement of these two pictures side by side is of interest for two reasons. Firstly they show two different techniques, and Turner's use of both watercolour and oil paint. Secondly they were painted at widely different times in his artistic development. Turner began as a topographical painter, working with the watercolourist Thomas Girtin (1775–1802). Together they travelled the country, recording their journeys in a series of delightful watercolour paintings. Turner painted this one while on a tour of Scotland in 1802.

The oil painting, painted some thirty years later, was so similar in composition that it may well have been based on the watercolour or studies for it. While the watercolour (above) represents the topographical thread of Turner's work, the oil painting (right) represents the emotional response to landscape that characterises his later work.

We do not feel we have to 'read' the oil painting as we might the watercolour. Turner's use of colour translates the experience of place direct; we feel we are there. The sense of place seems to come directly from our relationship to colour rather than to the objects themselves. Here the brush notes a tree or the tumult of water. It conjures a romantic illusion; Turner transforms the Falls of Clyde into a magical place.

Turner was a methodical worker, often painting many full-size 'drafts' to experiment with arrangements of colour. These paintings were for his own eyes only, but they formed the basis of his fine understanding of his own theories of colour. In later life he became a recluse, living and working alone but on his death the contents of his studio became the nation's property. The many fine oil paintings and full-size sketches can be seen in the Clore extension. Many of his watercolours are shown in the British Museum.

Turner became an artist early in life. It is often suggested that he could hardly write a grammatical sentence; yet his systematic study of colour over a long lifetime produced a language of visual beauty that perhaps surpassed that of all previous painting.

Project work

Produce a pair of landscape pictures. Both should be based on studies done out-of-doors. The first should be a topographical picture, a faithful record of what you can see. The second could be in a different medium, and can be based on an impression or an interpretation of what you have seen.

Soldiers

The Kensingtons at Laventie, 1915.
Eric Kennington (1888–1960).
Painting on glass, 137.2 × 160 cm.
Imperial War Museum, London.

'They stood miserably. They stretched encumbered limbs to take their rifles, listless, bemused, to slowly scrape away the thicker mire caked, with deadness in their eyes and hands as each to each they spake – like damned-corpse-gossiping of hopeless bleedin' dawns – then laugh to see themselves so straitened, tricked out in mudded stiffening. They beat against the padded walls to flow again the ebbing blood. They kicked the oozing sacks above the water surface till their toe-joints ached.' *In Parenthesis* by David Jones (1895–1974), written about his experience of the First World War.

Project work

Most families have someone with real experience of life in the armed forces. Find out from them what life was really like – not the high drama of battle, but the intimate detail, the routine, and the ritual of the soldier's life. A useful source of information might be the Burghclere Memorial Chapel decorated with mural paintings by Stanley Spencer.

Produce an extended piece of work based on the information you have discovered.

Edward Burra (1905–1976) lived near Rye on Romney Marsh in Kent. If you can find this area on the map you will see it is a bulge of land pointing towards France. In both world wars this country backwater became a vast military camp. The gravel beds and sheep pastures were criss-crossed with railway lines and hutted camps and every byway filled with soldiers, motivated by some strange purpose. Burra painted these men as strange creatures, aliens in a landscape, as they might appear to the country folk.

From the soldier's point of view, the First World War was the most horrific experience. If you have ever cause to doubt the extent of the slaughter then read the roll call of the dead on your local war memorial, or attend a service of remembrance in your local church when the names are read out.

For the first time in a major European conflict, the innocent citizen armies faced mass-produced industrialised death. The engineers produced guns of greater power, the chemists poison gases and ever more efficient explosives. Destruction took to the air and, in a foretaste of the Second World War, civilian targets were bombed. Against these awesome assaults soldiers placed their bodies, and in the macabre arithmetic of the High Commands, tried to absorb more bullets, shells and gas than the other side could produce. It was called a war of attrition.

It ended with millions dead, with mutinies in the armies, and an enduring horror that marked all those who took part in it. David Jones served in the trenches in this war and his book *In Parenthesis* is dedicated not only to his friends but to 'the enemy front-fighters who shared our pains'. For the soldiers, war itself became the enemy.

Soldiers at Rye, 1941.
Edward Burra (1905–1976).
Gouache and watercolour, 102.1 × 207 cm.
Tate Gallery, London.

Spring

Spring.
Jean-Francois Millet (1814–1875).
Oil on canvas, 86 × 111 cm.
Louvre Museum, Paris.

Millet's painting of 'Spring' (above), one of his last, is a marvellous evocation of the season. He painted many landscapes of rural France, usually built around the figures of peasant workers. The solid, solemn peasants that people pictures like 'The Gleaners' and 'The Angelus' stand in a flat landscape stretching to a distant horizon. 'Spring' is a real celebration of the season; in it he seems to rediscover the joy of paint, the sumptuous qualities that mark his early paintings of nudes.

Project work

Millet, and, after him, the Impressionists like Pissarro, were *plein-air* painters, working out-of-doors. Choose a landscape that appeals to you – not a grand view, but one of those forgotten corners that fill in the angles between buildings and the open spaces of the countryside. Paint or draw it, working on the spot.

Plum Trees in Blossom, 1894.
Camille Pissarro (1830–1903).
Oil on canvas, 61 × 74 cm.
Ordrupgaard Collection, Copenhagen.

Plein air is a term, meaning 'open air', used to describe paintings done out-of-doors. It seems such an obvious thing to do but until the early nineteenth century painting materials were too cumbersome to make it practical. Watercolours, of course, were an exception. Claude Monet (1840–1926), in his commitment to the idea, sometimes got carried away. One of his *plein air* paintings was so large that it had to be lowered into a trench so that he could complete the upper half.

Camille Pissarro was one the leading members of the Impressionist group. Some of his subject matter is like that of Millet: sturdy peasant folk going about their business. The painting above, of plum trees around his house at Eragny, reflects his abiding love of nature. He took great pleasure in these paintings of spring. He painted many including one in the company of Paul Cézanne, the two artists sitting side by side, painting the same view.

War

Wounded Guardsman, 1874.
Elizabeth Thompson (Lady Butler)
(1846–1933).
Oil on canvas.
National Army Museum, London.

Why do you think weapons are such popular children's toys? Do you think they glamorise violence? Do you think it is healthy to play games which feature violence and death? How much influence do you think television violence has on young children?

Make a survey of the types of children's toys that are available; you could use a home shopping catalogue as a source. Make a list of all the toys and give them a score according to the amount of violence they suggest.

Project work

Produce a set of work, supported by research, based on the way we commemorate our war dead. Almost every town and village has a war memorial; make sketches and studies based on yours.

or

Poppy day is traditionally the day on which we remember our war dead. It is marked by parades, poppy sellers, and wreaths on the Cenotaph. Use studies gathered on this day to produce a piece of work.

In the West, lack of familiarity with war in the last half of the twentieth century has again given rise to some of the romantic illusions that were common before the First World War. Children play war games and read war comics, guns are popular toys and in children's play, death and destruction are rehearsed.

It is true there is heroism, not only the dramatic but also the enduring heroism of ordinary people; nevertheless war is one of humanity's less praiseworthy activities.

Two Warriors' Heads, a drawing for 'The Battle of Anghiari', 1503.
Leonardo da Vinci (1452–1519).
Black and red chalk, 19.1 × 18.8 cm.
National Museum, Budapest.

A Warrior's Head, a drawing for 'The Battle of Anghiari', 1503.
Leonardo da Vinci (1452–1519).
Red chalk on pale, brown-toned paper,
22.6 × 18.6 cm.
National Museum, Budapest.

'You must make the conquered and beaten pale, their brows raised and knit, and the skin above their brows furrowed with pain, the sides of the nose with wrinkles going in an arch from the nostrils to the eyes, and make the nostrils drawn up and the lips arched upwards discovering the upper teeth; and the teeth apart as with crying out with lamentation ... You would see some of the victors leaving the fight and issuing from the crowd, rubbing their eyes and cheeks with both hands to clean them of the dirt made by their watering eyes smarting from the dust and the smoke.' Leonardo wrote this to describe his painting (now destroyed) of this battle.

Self-portrait

Self-portrait, 1889.
Vincent van Gogh (1853–1890).
Oil on canvas, 65 × 54 cm.
Musée d'Orsay, Paris.

Many artists have painted long series of self-portraits throughout their lives. Rembrandt van Rijn (1606–1669) painted a series that not only charts the changes in his appearance but also the changes in his style of painting. They have even been used as a yardstick to date his other work. The two paintings by Vincent van Gogh (1853–1890) illustrated here form part of a remarkable series that show the artist's struggle against the inevitable progress of his insanity.

Project work

Self-portraits are interesting in sequence. Find a series of self-portraits by a famous painter and see if you can describe how the style of execution changes. Rembrandt van Rijn is a good example.

Produce a self-portrait, as complete and as carefully executed as you can. Complete one at regular intervals during your course; it's a good habit to get into, and it will help you check your progress.

Van Gogh was never a successful artist during his lifetime, yet his work was of enormous influence on the painters who followed him. His work opened a channel which, through Fauvism, Expressionism and, eventually, Abstract Expressionism led to much which characterises painting today.

Portrait of the artist with bandaged ear, 1889.
Vincent van Gogh (1853–1890).
Oil on canvas, 60.5 × 50 cm.
Courtauld Collection, London.

Van Gogh cut off a part of his ear as a result of a quarrel with his friend and fellow painter Paul Gauguin (1848–1903). The portrait above was painted soon after he returned from hospital, his ear still bandaged. The handling of the paint seems to show his heightened state of excitement.

The self-portrait opposite is his last, completed just before he shot himself. The whole painting writhes: background, clothing and even the face twists and swirls. Only his piercing green eyes are still. Here the psychology of the painter seems revealed in his work.

Find and date as many of van Gogh's self-portraits as you can, and place them in order. How do you feel they compare with each other?

Mother and child

The Impressionist group included, quite unusually, women painters. In society, ladies with the ability to draw and even paint 'polite' watercolour subjects were quite acceptable. With music and conversation, it was a skill to be encouraged; but to take art seriously was frowned on, especially if you associated with unconventional characters like the painters of the Impressionist group. Berthe Morisot (1841–1895) became a friend of Manet, often his (decorously clothed) model, and eventually married his brother.

The Cradle 1873. *Berthe Morisot* (1841–1895). Oil on canvas, 56 × 46 cm. Louvre, Paris.

Project work

Painters have never been afraid to look to every-day life for their subject matter, but the Impressionist group, and perhaps in particular its women members, brought a new intimacy to the development of this theme.

Look to the everyday clutter of incidents that surround your daily routine. Find a subject and produce a series of pictures to reflect the normal rather than the extraordinary.

Berthe Morisot painted subjects drawn from experiences within her own circle, reflecting the domestic life of her time and in particular a woman's place in society.

The American artist, Mary Cassatt (1845–1926), was brought up in Europe. She settled in Paris in 1866 and began painting with the Impressionists. She was influenced by Degas (1834–1917) and by the art of the Japanese print, newly discovered by Europeans. She was best known for her pictures of mothers with children. Few of these pictures can be seen on this side of the Atlantic, but most major collections in the United States possess a painting or print by her. She saw her prints as a way of making art available to a wider audience and went to great lengths to make each print as individual as possible. As a result, many different colour schemes of the same design exist, for she often inked up the plates herself when experimenting with colours.

At the Window.
Mary Cassatt (1845–1926).
Pastel.
Musée d'Orsay, Paris.

Wealth

The Ambassadors, 1533.
Hans Holbein the Younger (1497–1543).
Oil on wood, 207 × 209.5 cm.
National Gallery, London.

Project work

The two pictures on these pages tell us, not only what people looked like, but by inference, a lot about their character.

Based on careful study, produce a portrait that describes your subject not only by appearance but by association. Surround your subject with evidence of interests and attainments.

Two young men, highly placed in the society of their age, stand surrounded by all the trappings of good taste and the attributes of intellectual attainment. This painting is a celebration, it is a bold announcement to the world that they have 'made it'. Mathematical and navigational instruments (the computer toys of their day!); fine books, carefully opened at significant texts; a lute; fine silks and rich jewellery complete the picture. Yet the whole is dominated by the distorted image of a skull, symbolic of the inevitability of death. The inclusion of a skull in a picture is a tradition found in many early portraits, perhaps a mark of humility to balance the vanity of having a portrait painted at all.

'The Ambassadors' may well have been designed to be seen from the right hand side, perhaps on stairs. The skull in the foreground can best be seen from a viewpoint low down on the right hand edge of the picture.

Hanson is unusual as a figurative sculptor in using his art form as social comment, and fairly savage at that. He focuses on all that seems in bad taste in dress, picking as his 'victims' middle-class Americans. The limits of this housewife's ambitions are to be seen in her bulging shopping trolley. No evidence of intellectual curiosity here.

The smooth skin-like texture that can be achieved with a material like fibreglass resin has led to others using it in figure work. John De Andreas (b. 1941) produces life-size nude figures in this technique. They are unsettling in their realism, unreal in their stillness.

The move towards realism in figurative sculpture has led to using actual people as 'living sculpture'. The artists Gilbert and George appeared as 'singing sculpture' in New York in 1971. Other artists have combined video, film, real and sculpted objects, and real people to make figurative sculpture into a moving, performing art.

Woman with a shopping cart.
Duane Hanson (b. 1925).
Real clothing and real objects over a fibre glass resin figure, 166 cm.
Neue Galerie, Aachen.

Madness

The Kleptomaniac.
Théodore Géricault (1791–1824).
Oil on canvas, 61.2 × 50.1 cm.
Gent Museum, Belgium.

Project work

We live in a world full of comfortable assumptions. We assume, for example, that the anonymous people who pass us by in the street are as interested in us as we are in them. The paranoid lives a life at the centre of the furtive and unwelcome attention of everyone. Innocent questions and actions are a threat to them and they feel enclosed and trapped.

Produce an extended set of work to describe the world as they might experience it.

Théodore Géricault (1791–1824) died aged thirty-two in a riding accident, his promise as an artist unfulfilled. All his life he searched for a subject worthy of his skills and talent. On the one occasion that he found such a subject and saw it through to completion, political cowardice on the part of the authorities it criticised denied him credit for it. This was 'The Raft of the Medusa', painted in 1819. It recorded the terrible events that took place after a shipwreck off the African coast.

It is ironic that his most complete cycle of works was painted not in search of a grand subject but as studies, portraits painted for a friend, a Dr Georget who cared for mentally deranged patients. These portraits date from an age when facial features were held to offer a view of one's personal characteristics. This idea was elevated to the status of a science, with books and diagrams written in its support.

Obsessive Envy.
Théodore Géricault (1791–1824).
Oil on canvas.
Musée des Beaux-Arts, Lyons,
France.

Phrenology, as it was called, was a study of the contours of the skull in order to determine a person's characteristics and talents. Criminal or insane tendencies could be diagnosed, it was believed, by measuring subject's skulls.

Physiognomy attempted to analyse facial shape in a similar way. Often a connection was made with the shapes of the faces of animals – people with sharp noses and narrow faces were said to be as cunning as foxes.

Both these psuedo-sciences have been long discredited but they were rife at the time Géricault painted these pictures for his friend Georget.

Originally, Géricault painted ten of these portraits for Georget; only five survive. The ten were painted to illustrate the ten obsessions that the doctor had identified in his book on mental illness. Dr Georget treated Géricault for depression, and the portraits were painted in gratitude though Géricault was always interested in human types – rather in the way Leonardo da Vinci collected grotesque subjects (see page 141).

Solitude

What we now call the Romantic movement in Art touched the artists of many countries. Their work is often characterised by a search for an unattainable ideal.

Samuel Palmer (1805–1881) painted the perfect vision of apple blossom, blossom in profusion. The silence of this garden seems heavy with its fragrance and the figure drifts through, a wraith at the end of the path. It is a picture for reflection. The figure walks as in a cloister, its progress stately.

Palmer was one of a group of artists who settled in the village of Shoreham in Kent. He and his companions sought to follow a life of simplicity, close to nature. The depth of silence in Palmer's pictures gives us some insight into the peace and tranquillity of pre-industrial England.

In a Shoreham Garden,
1830–35.
Samuel Palmer (1805–1881).
Watercolour and gouache,
27.9 × 22.1 cm.
Victoria and Albert Museum,
London.

Project work

All of us choose to be on our own at one time or another. Can you produce a piece of work, perhaps romantised or realistic, to reflect the way you use this solitude.

The terms 'Romanticism' and 'Realism' are often applied to the art of the earlier part of the nineteenth century. Very rough definitions are as follows: 'Romantic' artists tend to explore the world of dreams, to admire the dramatic and the heroic; 'Realist' artists are more concerned with the harsh realities of everyday life, with the circumstances of ordinary people – if they have heroes, these will often be workers, stoically engaged in back-breaking labour, rather than gorgeously-uniformed warriors brandishing gleaming sabres. Romanticism and Realism are much more complicated than this – in fact, they frequently overlap – but this explanation will do for our purpose.

Caspar David Friedrich (1774–1840) was the most prominent painter of the German Romantic School. His pictures reflected a spiritual view, an inner vision.

On a cold and misty morning the Romantic climbs to a hill-top and surveys the view. The Realist sees the damp, cold land, feels the ache of the climb and gasps at the raw air. The Romantic dreams of the hidden world beneath the mists.

The Wanderer above the Sea of Mist, 1810.
Caspar David Friedrich
(1774–1840).
Oil on canvas.
Kunsthalle, Hamburg.

Friedrich collected sketches, his own and those of others, often from different places and at different times, which he recreated in his imagination.

97

Death

This figure is from the tomb of René de Chalons. Through the coat of arms on his shield and the remnants of his rich cloak we can see it represents the young general in death; he was only twenty-six. The decaying corpse seems to offer his heart up to God. The sculpture dates from 1544, and the sculptor is thought to have been Ligier Richier (c.1500–1567).

The glorification of the dead was a major concern of Renaissance sculptors. Michelangelo Buonarroti (1475–1564) spent most of his working life worrying about his commission for the grandiose tomb of Pope Julius II. He called it the tragedy of his life. Julius commissioned Michelangelo to produce an extravagant tomb culminating in two figures: 'Heaven smiling, supporting a bier on her shoulder and the other, Cybele, the goddess of the Earth, who appeared grief-stricken at having to remain in a world robbed of all virtue through the death of such a great man.' Julius was as modest in death as he was peaceful in life. The tomb was never finished.

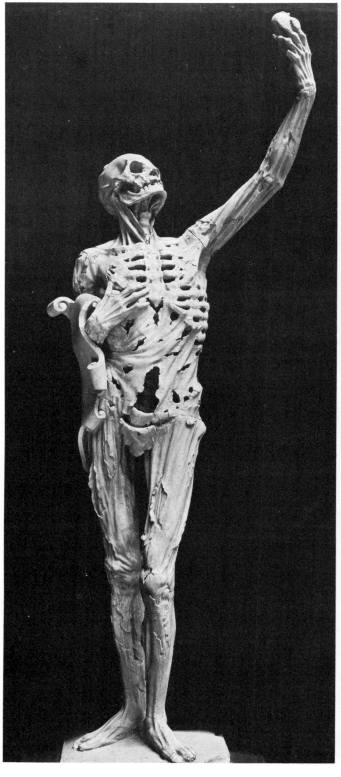

Tomb of René de Chalons.
Attributed to Ligier Richier (c.1500–1567).
Marble.
Bar-le-Duc, St Pierre.

Project work

The skull is often used in Renaissance portraits to symbolise the brevity of life. The death's head symbol is popular with some people to show their contempt for death. Make a series of studies based on the human skull. Use your studies as the basis for an extended piece of work.

In our culture we reject the idea of death, pushing it out of our minds, hiding it behind euphemisms. Perhaps we could accept it more easily if we talked about it.

A Dead Baby.
Samuel Cooper (1608–1672).
Black chalk with white, black and grey wash on pink washed paper, 14.8 × 18.6 cm.
Private collection.

From an age when infant mortality was an everyday occurrence, when children died at the rate common in the third world today, comes this sad drawing of a dead child. This was an age not too far distant: many older people who come from large families have lost brothers and sisters in childhood.

The picture is a fitting contrast to the horror of the tomb of René de Chalons. This is no rotting corpse; here the child sleeps. There is no pain, no fear, just a gentle passing away. The dead child stands for all the phrases we use to wrap up the stark fact of death: 'gone to Jesus', 'passed away', 'asleep', etc. The picture was commissioned by the child's parents, a last sad reminder of a lost life.

Still-life

Still-life is defined as a representation of a group of inanimate objects, traditionally those in everyday use. The wine bottles of the art room collection of still-life objects presumably belong to another tradition!

Still-Life with a Plaster Cupid.
Paul Cézanne (1839–1906).
Oil on canvas 70.6 × 57.3 cm.
Courtauld Collection, London.

An artist strives to understand and then to interpret and record what he or she has found. Often the problem of interpreting and recording complex three-dimensional objects on a two-dimensional picture surface requires careful investigation. Artists like Cézanne used still life to discover the way these problems of interpretation could be resolved. Cézanne developed the use of colour into a means of showing depth, rather than merely light and shade. He used thin touches of paint, placed side by side, so that the differences of colour and tone give the effect of three-dimensions.

Project work

Produce an in-depth study of a group of objects. Treat your work as an investigation – a study in attaining an illusion of depth on a flat picture surface. Try to look beyond the idea of a representation of the objects, to show more than can be seen from one viewpoint.

Still-Life with a Water Jug, 1893.
Paul Cézanne (1839–1906).
Oil on canvas, 53.3 × 71.1 cm.
Tate Gallery, London.

Cézanne also used the white of his prepared canvas rather as a watercolour painter uses the white of the paper, not only allowing its luminosity to come through veils of paint, but also often leaving areas of the canvas unpainted between the strokes of colour, and seeming sometimes to have left the painting unfinished.

He was a slow, rather laborious worker who found the spontaneity of his Impressionist contemporaries an impossible method of working. He turned to still-life as a manageable and controllable subject, a subject which, unlike his landscapes, he could walk around and rearrange. Through his still-life paintings he developed the vocabulary to work on his great landscape studies of L'Estaque and Mont St Victoire. His analysis of structure, of volume, made possible by the rigour of his studies, was his contribution to the development of Art.

Dance

Project work

Produce an extended set of work, or a series of sketch-book studies based on your observations of athletes at rest, either after a game or during an interval. Try to capture the relaxed poses or the exercises they use to 'warm up' and keep supple. Your work might be collected over a period of time.

Edgar Degas (1834–1917) used his knowledge and love of the ballet as a theme in his work over a period of many years. His paintings, sketches and sculpture all show the acute sense of observation which he brought to bear on his work. His sketches, like the two illustrated here, capture dancers in unguarded and unposed moments. They are often masterpieces in their own right.

Dancer Adjusting Her Slipper.
Edgar Degas (1834–1917).
Pastel.
Lexbourne Ltd., London.

Degas was influenced by the comparatively recently-discovered art of photography in his daring compositions, which reflected the spontaneous unposed image that the camera could achieve.

Dancer.
Edgar Degas (1834–1917).
Sketch in oils on pink paper.
Louvre, Paris.

Peace

Le Déjeuner sur l'Herbe, 1863.
Edouard Manet (1832–1883).
Oil on canvas, 215 × 270 cm.
Louvre, Paris.

Project work

These three pictures show the fine 'tuning' that an artist can undertake to complete a work of importance. The subject is a picnic. Use this as a source for a composition of your own. It will require some careful figure studies.

The tranquillity of this subject was in sharp contrast to the response it got at its official unveiling. When it first appeared it was pilloried by the critics and even the Emperor expressed his shock at seeing it. This fact alone made it instantly *the* picture to be seen, and thousands flocked to see it and be similarly shocked. What assaulted the taste of the time, nurtured on nudity in pictures presented in classical guise and therefore acceptable, was the lack of any such legitimising context. The dress of the men was the dress of modern-day France; that, and the bold, unembarrassed stare of their naked female companion was too much for polite French society to take.

The version below, which hangs in the Courtauld Gallery in London, was painted after the Louvre painting, possibly to hang in a smaller room. Painted in a freer style and with a more brightly-lit effect, it may have been painted after a considerable interval. As it was painted for a friend, it may well represent a more private, personal interpretation of the theme.

Le Déjeuner sur l'Herbe,
*c.*1863.
Edouard Manet (1832–1883).
Oil on canvas, 89.5 × 116.5 cm.
Courtauld Collection, London.

Le Déjeuner sur l'Herbe, 1863.
Edouard Manet (1832–1883).
Pen, ink, watercolour over black chalk, 40.8 × 48 cm.
Ashmolean Museum, Oxford.

The version in the Ashmolean may well be a sketch of the Louvre version. X-ray studies show the Louvre painting to have been altered many times by the artist, while the two pictures in this country reflect the finished composition, suggesting that they came after it.

Power (I)

Power is defined as the ability to act and to persuade or force others to act for you.

Officer Charging, 1812.
Théodore Géricault (1791–1824).
Oil on canvas.
Christie's, London.

The latter half of the eighteenth century and the early years of nineteenth century were a time of war in Europe. Military uniforms were developed in a style as Romantic as the times. The officer in this painting by Géricault is a hero (his pose tells you so). The strong diagonal of the charging horse, the slash of the sabre and his warlike expression mark him out as a man of courage.

Napoleon Bonaparte came to power in France and brought some kind of order after the upheavals of the French Revolution. He saw the propaganda value of art, and he used painters to project an impression of him as a 'hero', a 'superman'. Again and again paintings appear that glorify him. In this he was little different from the kings who preceded him, but he was perhaps more fortunate in his choice of artists.

Project work

People who wish to appear important use similar devices today. Politicians who are not popular try to be seen with film stars or brave people who are. Produce an extended set of work, supported by studies, to project yourself as a person of power.

The low viewpoint used by these two artists creates an illusion of size and of grandeur. Their subjects are made to appear larger than life.

Napoleon crossing the Alps.
Jacques-Louis David (1748–1825).
Oil on canvas, 96 × 91 cm.
Charlottenburg Castle, Berlin.

Jacques-Louis David was one of the greatest painters of his age. He chose classical themes which supported his political ideas. 'The Oath of the Horatii' reflects his belief that service to the state is the highest ideal. When he turned to his own time for subject matter, it was to support his masters in power.

If you look at the rocks in the foreground of the picture above you will see the names of the

conquerors that crossed the Alps before Napoleon. Hannibal's name, though faded by age, can be read. Karolus Magnus refers to Charlemagne, a great hero of the French and the Emperor of the Holy Roman Empire. Bonaparte's name has been deliberately placed alongside them.

David's work for Napoleon culminates in the vast painting, now in the Louvre, 'The Coronation of Napoleon', 1805–1807. It depicts the Emperor, surrounded by his generals, his family (many of whom he made kings and princes), and by all the power of his Empire. Having taken it from the hands of the Pope, Napoleon lifts the crown to his own head, perhaps implying that no mere mortal is important enough to do this for him.

Autumn

Damp Autumn, 1941.
Ivon Hitchins (1893–1979).
Oil on canvas, 40.6 × 74.3 cm.
Tate Gallery, London.

The beauty of autumn is in its colours. We feel surprise each year when the accepted, ignored greens, so taken for granted, suddenly become reds, golds, oranges and browns. The differences in colour and tone of the foliage in autumn have far more contrast than the summer colours.

Ivon Hitchens (1893–1979) developed a distinctive landscape style, close to abstraction, of which the painting above is a typical example. Broad brushstrokes in naturalistic colours describe the British autumn day, the liquidity of the paint an apt reflection of our autumn weather. Autumn trees drip with the dampness of rain and the condensation of early morning mists, the landscape seen as through a veil of vapourish air. Hitchin's work developed in a more and more abstract style, eventually leaving behind natural colours and using bright mauves, reds and yellows.

Project work

Produce a set of work, based on observation, of the changes that occur as autumn sets in. Your work could consist not only of drawn records but also of interesting objects collected and imaginatively presented.

Autumn Leaves, 1855/56.
Sir John Everett Millais (1829–1896).
Oil on canvas.
Manchester City Art Gallery.

Millais' painting of autumn leaves looks beyond the narrative for a deeper significance in the season. The figures are those of his daughters and their two friends. Sombrely dressed, they pour gold and orange leaves into their basket. Autumn in their hands seems rich, the leaves like jewels or fragments of gold. The children with their futures gather up the riches of the past.

Millais, with William Holman Hunt (1827–1910) and Dante Gabriel Rossetti (1828–1882), formed a group of artists known as the Pre-Raphaelite Brotherhood. This group sought to distance itself from what they saw as the trivial incidents and the pretentious history pictures that characterised official, academy art. They tried to re-create the simplicity of purpose which they felt characterised the work of the Early Renaissance painters – those before Raphael (1483–1520).

Their insistence on subject matter with a moral or instructive purpose, their attention to detail – especially observed in nature – and their use of bright colours immediately marked them out as different from the 'official' painters. It took the interest and support of the writer and critic John Ruskin (1819–1900) to gain the group recognition.

The early lack of official recognition for the Pre-Raphaelites made their work more available to the 'new' rich, the manufacturers of the North of England who were more susceptible to new ideas and whose philanthropy gave the best of their pictures to the new galleries in their home towns. Birmingham, Manchester and other places in the industrial north have by far the most comprehensive collections of these artists' works.

Theatre

Noctes Ambrosianae, 1906.
Walter Richard Sickert (1860–1942).
Oil on canvas, 63.5 × 76.2 cm.
Nottingham Castle Museum.

Walter Sickert (1860–1942) was one of the major influences on British art in this century. He formed the Fitzroy Street Group as a way of spreading his view of the place of art in society. This group of artists met in Sickert's lodgings in Fitzroy Street to talk about and display their work. It evolved into the Camden Town Group which continued its influence until 1913. Sickert concentrated on a professional and systematic approach to his art. This was well suited to the group's no-nonsense choice of subject matter – the urban, the ordinary, real world, all hints of the artificial removed.

Sickert had the ability to catch the 'moment' in his work, the essentials of any scene. In his theatre crowds each face is rapt with attention. In his later society portraits he has caught an almost photographic feel of immediacy and an impressive degree of characterisation.

Project work

Observe the way theatre lighting affects a scene. If you have access to a hall or stage with special lighting set up, you could experiment with these effects. You can try out different effects using slides of coloured gel. Prepare an extended piece of work based either on a still-life or on figure studies under your own planned lighting.

The Old Bedford, 1897.
Walter Richard Sickert (1860–1942).
Oil on canvas, 76.2 × 60.2 cm.
Walker Art Gallery, Liverpool.

The New Bedford, *c.*1915/16.
Walter Richard Sickert (1860–1942).
Tempera and oil on canvas, 185.5 × 72.4 cm.
Leeds City Art Gallery.

Sickert was a great lover of the music hall, the variety theatre of his day. This group of paintings is one of the pillars on which his reputation rests. Here is a body of work as broad and consistent as the work of Degas, to whose influence he owed a great deal. Sickert, like Degas frequently made use of photographic sources for his work. They were both fascinated by the richness of the architecture and the dramatic lighting of the theatre. Sickert's music hall paintings directly correspond to the later cabaret and café-concert themes of his French contemporaries.

Summer

Bathers, Asnières, 1883/84.
Georges-Pierre Seurat (1859–1891).
Oil on canvas, 201 × 300 cm.
National Gallery, London.

Georges-Pierre Seurat was one of the most influential painters of the nineteenth century. His scientific, methodical approach to his work set him apart from his more expressionist contemporaries, Vincent van Gogh (1853–1890) and Paul Gauguin (1848–1903). Seurat died young but his painting of the bathers shows how impressive his attainment nevertheless was. This monumental composition with its clear atmosphere typifies the stillness of a hot summer's afternoon.

Seurat made studies of the old masters and of the great painters of the more immediate past, Ingres (1780–1867) and Delacroix (1798–1863) for example. Evidence of this close study can be seen in the deliberate construction of this picture. He developed a style of painting, known as 'pointillism', a style he developed as a result of his study of the way Delacroix used colour and the colour theories of Chevreul (a chemist who wrote an influential treatise on colour). He added this technique to this painting in 1887. See the red hat of the boy in the water, for example.

Project work

Place dots of pure colour next to each other in different combinations to create changes in tone and, through that, form. You might do this in the form of completed strips.

Use the information you have gained from your experiments to create a composition based on the theme of swimming.

The Gleaner, *c.*1882.
Georges-Pierre Seurat (1859–1891).
Conte crayon, 32 × 24 cm.
British Museum, London.

Seurat's tonal drawings are as interesting and as individual as his paintings. They show the same depth of study and the same methodical approach. Many of his drawings take the form of studies for his paintings. He worked out the designs for his few large paintings in great detail. His drawings worked out the tonal qualities and the compositional balance he sought. He drew individual figures and then, finally, sketches of the whole composition before 'squaring up' to transfer it to the canvas.

An interesting aspect of his work is the painted frames which enclose some of his pictures. In some of his work there is also a painted border to the picture, forming a margin on the canvas itself. The frames and borders are in the same pointillist style as the subject. They were such a distinctive feature of his work that borders and frames were often added by another hand at a later date ('The Circus', 1891 – The Louvre, Paris).

Seurat directly influenced a small group of painters, notably Paul Signac (1863–1935), who wrote an important analysis of Seurat's theories. Henri Matisse (1869–1954) was profoundly influenced by meeting Signac.

Power (II)

Emperor Vitellius.
Jacopo Tintoretto (1518–1594).
Black chalk with white on blue
paper, 28.2 × 32 cm.
Staatliche Graphische Sammlung,
Munich.

There is a story that when Tintoretto, who was a Venetian artist of the sixteenth century, was asked how to become a great artist he replied, 'draw, draw, draw'. The drawing of the Emperor Vitellius, drawn from a piece of classical Roman sculpture, represents the results of his philosophy. Roman Emperors were not normally known for peaceful lives. Could you guess at the Emperor's character from this drawing? Do you think he was a man who enjoyed using his power?

Project work

Produce an extended piece of work based on the idea of power and its effects on those who exercise it and on those who serve them.

The tyrants of Ancient Greece, the Emperors of Rome, Chinese Emperors and many others held absolute power: the power of life and death, the licence to act upon a whim and affect the lives of thousands. To be successful, their power often depended upon military strength and upon the fear this instilled. The (fortunately short-lived) Emperor of Haiti, Henry I, marched companies of soldiers off the ramparts of his castle just to impress his European visitors. The fragility of power based on this kind of fear is demonstrated by his eventual fate which was to commit suicide when his army rebelled. The modern world sets limits to the power of any one person, a system of checks and balances which we call democracy. It is our antidote to the theory that while 'power corrupts, absolute power corrupts absolutely'.

114

Detail of Colleoni Equestrian Statue.
Andrea del Verrocchio (1435–1488).
Bronze, height of statue:
3.95 metres.
Venice, Italy.

Find out all you can about the way power is used in your community; talk to elected representatives and to local officials. Why do you think the exercise of power is so fascinating to watch, even when so transparently dramatised as in television soap opera?

This is a detail from the Colleoni equestrian statue by Andrea del Verrochio (1435–1488). It was erected by the state of Venice as a tribute to one of its military leaders. The fierce expression and hard stare of a ruthless man glare down across a Venetian square. The power of his expression is in its exaggeration, almost to the point of caricature. This is the face of war. Perhaps it is all the more surprising to learn that Colleoni was a patron of the arts. The statue was a technical masterpiece – the horse and rider both cast in bronze. The equestrian portrait, directly derived from the Roman portraits of emperors, is a form that has come down to us in this century. Military leaders from the First and Second World Wars sit, often ill at ease, recorded for the future on horseback.

Famous pictorial examples from earlier times are the Titian (*c.*1487/90–1576) portrait of Charles V on horseback, and the painting by van Dyck (1599–1641) of our own Charles I (in the National Gallery, London). See if you can find these or any other examples. Can you think of reasons why this form of portrait was so popular with leaders? Would you consider this to be a suitable way for current political leaders to be portrayed?

Alone

The Scream, 1893.
Edvard Munch (1863–1944).
Oil on canvas, 90.8 × 73.6 cm.
National Gallery, Oslo.

Project work

Produce an extended set of work, supported by appropriate research, based on the idea of being alone; consider the unwilling isolation of the mentally ill, of prisoners, the disabled, the old and the sick.

'The Scream' is an image much used by Munch in his work. The isolated figure on the bridge screams and the sky vibrates to his cry. Along the solid bridge come two more distant figures, their hard sillouettes increasing the air of menace and emphasising the isolation of the terrified person in the foreground.

The painting is based on a frightening experience felt one evening while Munch was out for a walk. It is a reflection of Munch's own melancholy life, yet it seems to strike a chord with all of us: it is surprisingly popular, often sold in reproduction.

Portrait of an Unknown Man, *c.*1588.
Nicholas Hilliard (1547–1619).
Oil, 13 × 6 cm.
Victoria and Albert Museum, London.

Student's work.

Contrast the frantic isolation of the figure in Munch's picture with the calm resignation of the young man in the miniature by Hilliard. Miniature portraits, the art of the limner, were often tokens of love and affection. They were either mounted in lockets or worn on chains. The symbols that surround the unknown young man in this portrait suggest that the love he felt was not returned. The tangle of roses and briars, sweet but wrapped in thorns, suggest that the path of love was less than smooth. The quality of the portrait as an expression of feeling is strong, yet far more subtle than the bludgeon Munch uses to assault our feelings. Yet, for all its calm, Hilliard's figure is no less alone.

We live lives increasingly crowded. Even when we seek to get away, to be alone, we find crowds motivated by a similar need. In the summer some of the remotest parts of our island have roads choked with visitors and footpaths collapsing with over-use. Soon we may find being alone, away from the sounds of our fellow humans, difficult to achieve. The need for peace, for the quiet to enjoy reflection, is essential to the human spirit.

Is this a need you have felt? Have you ever been truly alone or does the prospect frighten you? Have you ever felt the loss of love or the need to scream with Munch? Can you describe how you felt?

117

Seeing

The Farm Gate, 1950.
Stanley Spencer (1891–1959).
Oil on canvas, 88.9 × 57.2 cm.
Royal Academy of Arts,
London.

Stanley Spencer (1891–1959) was brought up in the rural peace of the village of Cookham in Berkshire. It is often his life in the village that is recorded in his pictures. He loved to use it as a background for many of the visionary and religious paintings that make up the main body of his work.

Cows at Cookham, 1936.
Stanley Spencer (1891–1959).
Oil on canvas, 76.2 × 50.8 cm.
Ashmolean Museum, Oxford.

Project work

The camera enables us to catch moments like these, but unless you are fortunate they seldom appear in such a convenient compositional form. Take some photographs to support your observations of people in public places. In the studio, consider a pictorial arrangement that might fit all or some of your figures.

Make a picture or a series of pictures that fuse the immediate camera image with your organisational skill as an artist.

Spencer also painted scenes from the everyday life of the village, real or imagined. His contribution to landscape painting rests on a series of paintings of Cookham village. The two paintings here show his rich vein of invention and his compositional sense. In the boy latching the gate and the child reaching for the dandelion clock we have two incidents that show the sharpness of his observation. His sense of composition is strong and dramatic, with no inhibitions about the unusual viewpoint. These two works show he has the important qualities of any great artist: the ability to see and then to organise what he has seen.

119

Travel

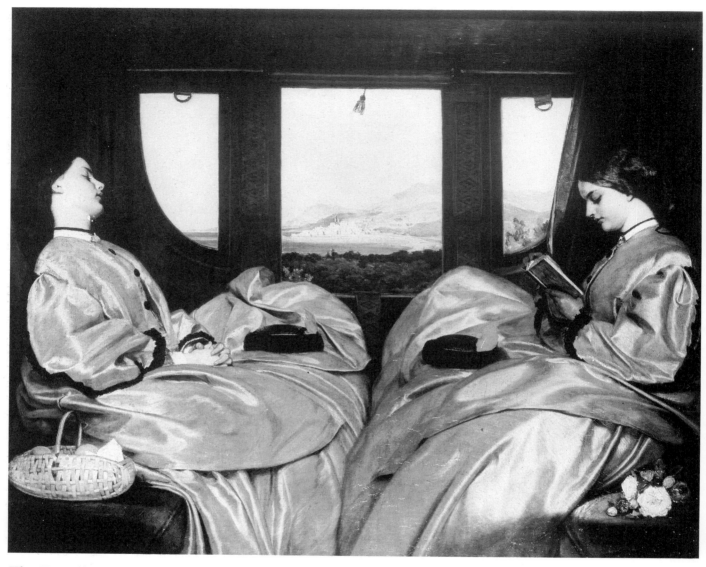

The Travelling Companions, 1862.
Augustus Leopold Egg, RA (1816–1863).
Oil on canvas, 64.1 × 76.2 cm.
Birmingham City Art Gallery.

The Victorian artists were as impressed as anyone by the novelty of convenient transport. Before the advent of the railway, public transport was by barge, by carrier's wagon or by coach. This was a slow and cumbersome process. The railways opened up travel for all.

The painting above is an example of a Victorian painter showing off, a *tour de force*. The painting of the satin dresses and the landscape through the carriage windows are examples of the skill of the artist. The subject, two English ladies travelling by train through the Italian countryside, shows that the 'Grand Tour', without which no aristocrat's education was complete, was now within the reach of the new rich. The age of mass tourism was at hand!

Find out what you can about the 'Grand Tour' and its effects on British Art, in particular on our art collections.

Omnibus Life in London, 1859.
William Maw Egley (1826–1916).
Oil on canvas, 44.8 × 41.9 cm.
Tate Gallery, London.

William Maw Egley's painting of the interior of a London Bus in mid-nineteenth century, is a straight-forward narrative picture. It presents the bus as an interesting technological invention. The idea of travelling with people other than family or friends was a novel one. Public transport, now taken so much for granted, was then a curiosity. What do you suppose the painter would have made of the London Underground?

Project work

Make a survey of the way public transport is used in your area. What sort of 'mixed bag' are its customers? You could make a series of sketches during a bus journey, a unique record of the passengers and the scenery. You could use photographic evidence as a part of your study.
or
Consider the view of the world you might get from the upper deck of a double-decker bus. With photographs and through sketches, prepare a piece of work that reflects this bird's-eye view.

Grief

Project work

Sadness and grief are as much a part of human experience as happiness and joy.

Produce an extended piece of work based on an unhappy experience you might have had. Try and give us a glimpse of what you thought and what you felt like. Help us to understand your experience.

Often we do not like to talk about our sorrows, and if you do not want to, you do not have to tackle this question. However, talking, writing or drawing about a problem often helps you to comes to terms with it.

The free brushwork and use of colour set Munch apart from the rather academic paintings that were in the majority in the later part of the nineteenth century, before the work of the Post-Impressionist painters had been fully assimilated. His uncompromising content and style stimulated a whole new movement in art (though there are, of course, many earlier examples of melancholy subject matter).

The Sick Child, 1907.
Edvard Munch (1863–1944).
Oil on canvas, 118.7 × 121 cm.
Tate Gallery, London.

Grief is one of our strongest emotions, and one we will all, sooner or later, share. Edvard Munch (1863–1944) painted many versions of the death of his sister. The picture opposite is the fourth of six painted versions that share the same composition. Munch was determined to paint life's unhappier side; he apparently abhorred the cosy domestic interiors that it was generally fashionable to paint. He preferred human content in his pictures and chose to paint people at their most emotional: in love, happy or sad, but seldom simply passive.

He had a complicated family life as a child and this seems to be reflected in his paintings.

Munch was a Norwegian artist whose glimpses into the darker side of human experience influenced the mainly Germanic group of painters known as the Expressionists. As we have seen (page 116), his unhappy subjects are surprisingly popular, and reproductions of his work sell well. Perhaps, rather like our appreciation of a cruel joke, we are relieved that the predicaments he depicts affect others rather than ourselves.

By the Death Bed, 1895.
Edvard Munch (1863–1944).
Oil on canvas, 149.9 × 167.6 cm.
Rasmus Meyer Collection, Bergen.

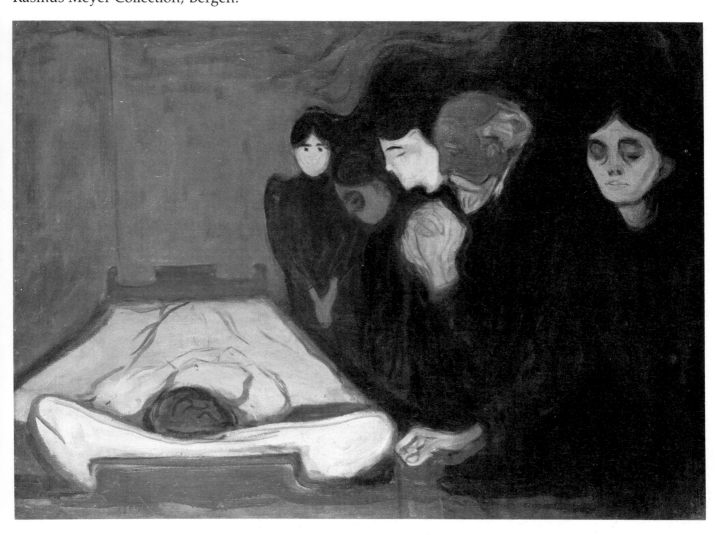

Cabaret

**'Moulin Rouge: La Goulue':
Study for a Poster**, 1891.
Henri de Toulouse-Lautrec
(1864–1901).
154 × 118 cm.
Musée Toulouse-Lautrec, Albi.

Toulouse-Lautrec was probably the greatest and one of the first artists to elevate the design of the poster into an art form in its own right. He designed twenty-eight posters in a style as new and exciting as the times they celebrated.

Deformed and stunted by an accident in childhood, which contributed to his early death at the age of thirty-seven, he found acceptance in the 'low life' of Paris. Singers, dancers and chorus girls, prostitutes and their clients were all subject to the penetrating, incisive lines of his art.

Project work

Live entertainment is still alive today. Search it out and make studies of street theatre, buskers or street musicians. From your studies design and, if you have the facilities, print a poster.

Yvette Guilbert: Study for a Poster, 1894.
Henri de Toulouse-Lautrec
(1864–1901).
186 × 93 cm.
Musée Toulouse-Lautrec, Albi.

Toulouse-Lautrec was subject to influences parallel to those that shaped the art of Edgar Degas (1834–1917). He was an enthusiast of the new art of photography. He experimented with combinations of oil paint and pastel as did Degas. Often his subject matter and low, informal viewpoint are reminiscent of the latter's work. Toulouse-Lautrec was his own man, however, and the style and vividness that he brought to the art of colour lithography sets him out as an innovator of greatness.

Inspiration for his printing came in part from the Japanese woodblock prints which were popular in Paris at the time. By the mid-nineteenth century Japan was emerging from centuries of self-imposed isolation and its culture had a dramatic impact on the European world. Find for yourself some examples of Japanese woodblock prints. You might like to compare them with the complex engravings of a European like Gustave Doré (1832–83).

Captives

Michelangelo was for forty years imprisoned by the commission he accepted from Pope Julius II for the pontiff's tomb. The Pope harried and pestered Michelangelo to finish the tomb while he was still alive. Eventually only the figure of Moses was carved by his own hand. The rest of the tomb, much smaller than was originally planned was completed by assistants.

Project work

Contorted figures writhe to escape their chains. They were to represent those captured in battle by the far-from peaceful Pope Julius II. Produce a series of figure studies to illustrate the captive theme.

These three incomplete figures were once to be part of the tomb of Julius II. They can now be found in the Accademia in Florence, and they demonstrate the method of carving used by Michelangelo.

Wax figures, fully modelled and in the round, were placed in a bath of water. The water's surface was, of course, horizontal. The figure was then slowly raised out of the water. As the figure was revealed, so, guided by its contours, the artist carved. Experiment with water and a lay figure or a doll, and you will see how this was done.

This may partly explain the finished state of those parts of the carving closest to the viewer, and the rough unhewn state of the marble from which the figure seems to emerge. It helps to give the impression that the figures are held captive by the stone, their struggle to escape mirroring the artist's struggle to create.

Michelangelo is often thought of as the pre-eminent artist of the Italian Renaissance. Painter of the vast Sistine Chapel ceiling, architect of St Peter's basilica in Rome, sculptor of the figure of David, the symbol of his home city of Florence.

Find out all you can about these three works, some of the most enduring monuments of their age.

Captives: Awakening Giant.
Michelangelo Buonarroti (1475–1564).
Marble.
Accademia, Florence, Italy.

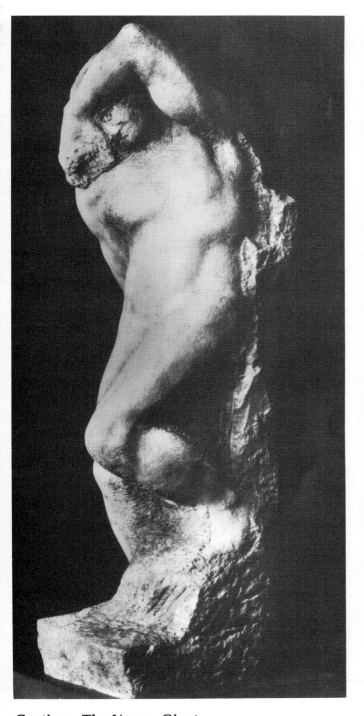

Captives: The Young Giant.
Michelangelo Buonarroti (1475–1564).
Marble.
Accademia, Florence, Italy.

Captives: Bearded Slave.
Michelangelo Buonarroti (1475–1564).
Marble.
Accademia, Florence, Italy.

Pageant

Two Heralds in Ceremonial Dress, Figures from a Procession of the Order of the Garter, St George's Day.
Sir Peter Lely (1618–1680).
Black and white chalk on blue paper, 51.8 × 36.4 cm.
Courtauld Collection, London.

Project work

Pageantry and procession are things we love to see. From the informality of the carnival to the formality of a royal occasion, processions have been developed as spectacles to impress and to be enjoyed.

Produce a series of paintings, drawings or other works showing scenes from such an event.

These two drawings are part of the thirty-one surviving drawings of a series to mark the annual St George's Day Procession. It takes place on 23 April to this day. It is interesting to compare this set with the drawings done by Feliks Topolski (b. 1907) to record the coronation in 1953.

Charles II reinstated the Order of the Garter when he was restored to the throne of England. Find out what you can about this very old order of chivalry.

The pageantry and splendour of the occasion reflected the resurgence of royalist feelings in the country. There is no evidence that these drawings were studies for a larger work, though Lely may have hoped for such a commission. The drawings are finished works, some actually portraits. Others in an unfinished state may well have been waiting for a sitting to finish them. The unfinished herald is a case in point.

In 1953, Feliks Topolski produced a set of drawings to record the coronation of Queen Elizabeth II. He was appointed official artist. In 1959 he was given a commission to turn these drawings into the Coronation Panorama which hangs in Buckingham Palace.

Can you think of other types of pageants from your own experience? Perhaps you have visited a carnival procession or the Lord Mayor's Show in London. Some costumes in use on civic occasions were designed to support pageantry – the uniforms of the Yoeman of the Guard or the Trumpeters at state occasions are examples of this. Try to imagine what state occasions or carnivals would be like without the brilliantly-coloured dress uniforms and costumes.

A Canopy-Bearer, Figure from the Procession of the Order of the Garter, St George's Day.
Sir Peter Lely (1618–1680).
Chalk on blue-grey paper, 49.8 × 23.5 cm.
British Museum, London.

Work

Coalbrookdale by Night, 1801.
Philip de Loutherbourg (1740–1812).
Oil on canvas, 67.9 × 106.7 cm.
Science Museum, London.

These two pictures span the industrial revolution in Britain. When de Loutherbourg painted Coalbrookdale he painted a novelty, a curiosity. No doubt aided by his experience as a painter of theatrical backdrops, with his eye for dramatic effect, his painting records early industry in a hitherto entirely agricultural land.

Gilbert Spencer (who was the brother of Stanley Spencer) also paints a curiosity, the last surviving flutter of pre-industrial agriculture. After the Second World War, with its unprecedented demands on home-grown food, the horse virtually disappeared from the countryside. It can be seen again today, but only rarely and often as a museum showpiece.

The folk song, some of whose verses are printed on the page opposite, reflects the pressure working people were under at that time of great change we know as the Industrial Revolution. The revolution changed the face of the British landscape as well as the lives of its people.

Project work

Work in the town and in the country has changed beyond imagination over the last forty years. Collect evidence, either drawn or photographic, that will help you either show some aspect of the past, record some aspect of the present, or project some imaginary vision of the future.

Cotswold Farm, 1931.
Gilbert Spencer (1892–1979).
Oil on canvas, 141 × 184.3 cm.
Tate Gallery, London.

The Dalesman's Litany (traditional)

It's hard when folks can't find no work
where they were bred and born.
When I was young I always thought
I'd bide mid stooks of corn.
But I've been forced to work in towns,
so here's my litany; from Hull and Halifax
and Hell –
Good Lord Deliver Me.

I've worked in Leeds and Huddersfield
and I've earn't some honest brass.
In Bradford, Keighley, Rotherham
I've fed me bairns and lass.
I've travelled all three Ridings round
and once I went to sea.
From forges, mills and coaling boats –
Good Lord Deliver Me.

I've walked at night through Sheffield town
it was just like being in Hell.
Where furnaces thrust out tongues of fire
and roared like the winds off the fells.
I've sent up coals in Barnsley's pits
with mud up to my knees.
From Barnsley, Sheffield, Rotherham –
Good Lord Deliver Me.

But now the children are all gone
to the country I've come back.
There's forty miles of heathery moor
twixt us and the coal pit stacks.
And as I sit by the fire at night
in rural poverty,
from Hull and Halifax and Hell –
The Good Lord Delivered Me.

131

Winter

Claude Monet (1840–1926) was the painter who above all gave Impressionism credibility as a school of painting. Totally committed to painting in the open air, even his snow scenes were worked on out-of-doors. Others before the Impressionists had worked out of doors, but this is an idea that we take for granted now because of the work of the artists of the Impressionist group; it is hard for us to imagine any other way to work, yet even great contemporaries of Monet like Edouard Manet (1832–1883) painted for many years in the studio only. In 1874 he is recorded as joining Monet at his home in Argenteuil to paint in the open air, an event thought unusual enough to be worth noting!

Project work

Produce an extended set of work to act as a record of winter. Collect drawings, photographs, etc. of scenes you see as typical. Use them as a source of your work.

or

Wait for the snow, the cold winds and the slush, wrap up warm and find out for yourself the problems that beset Monet as a *plein air* painter of snow scenes.

The Magpie.
Claude Monet (1840–1926).
Oil on canvas.
Musée de l'Orangerie, Paris.

As is often the case, the term Impressionism was coined by critics more interested in being unkind than in being constructive. Monet and other like-minded artists sought an interpretation of reality with as much vigour as the official painters of the salon. Their concentration on the effects of light was an important aspect of this search.

Monet painted many great series of paintings, subjects often chosen for their atmospheric qualities. The façade of Rouen Cathedral inspired a great series of twenty pictures which explored the effects of light on its carved, encrusted face. Other subjects he chose were: empty railway stations filled with steam and light, the play of light on water, seascapes, and haystacks.

Snow scenes occupied a central part of his repertoire. The two pictures here demonstrate their quality. Monet brought to these two paintings the keenness of observation that characterises his work. Here in the shadows can be found the lightness of touch that gives Monet's snow its feathery quality.

Monet had a remarkably long working life that began with his revolutionary work against the representatives of official art, and ended with his celebrated water-lilies series of paintings. When he died in 1926 the world of art had changed irrevocably and the direction of that change was in no small measure due to him. Cubism, Fauvism, Expressionism, a world war and an economic depression had all passed him by. His later paintings, the water-lilies, are a direct development of his Impressionist work: he was no follower of fashion. He remained true to his creed until the end.

Sunshine and Snow, Lavancourt, 1881.
Claude Monet (1840–1926).
Oil on canvas, 59.5 × 81 cm.
National Gallery, London.

Persecution

Converted British Family Sheltering a Christian Priest from the Persecution of the Druids, 1850.
William Holman Hunt (1827–1910).
Oil on canvas, 110.5 × 133.4 cm.
Ashmolean Museum, Oxford.

To persecute is to persist in ill-treatment or harassment of a person or group, often of persons of another race or religion or of opposing political persuasion.

In the early Roman Empire, Christians were seen as a threat to the power of the Emperors. They were different, and they seemed to pose a threat, so they were persecuted. Often they were thrown into the arena to be eaten by wild animals for the amusement of the crowds. Gradually they achieved acceptance, as many important citizens and eventually the Emperor himself became Christians. Secure in the official faith of the Empire, Christians in their turn set about persecuting the sects and heretics they found among their number.

Project work

Some minority groups feel they are persecuted in our society today. Try and define the form this persecution might take. Do you have any direct experience of it?

Produce a piece of work that describes some form of persecution in our society today.

Minorities have often found themselves in difficulties – many of the conflicts in the world today are on racial or religious grounds. In this country ethnic minorities often feel they are persecuted by an uncaring society ignorant of their culture and their needs.

Deportation to Death, 1945.
Leopold Mendez.
Linocut.
Musée de l'Art Moderne, Paris.

The Jewish race have been persecuted for centuries. Traditionally, cynical rulers have blamed them for the problems of their state. In Eastern Europe until the later half of this century they were forced to live apart from the gentile population. They lived in walled areas called ghettos.

In Germany, after the First World War, the country was in chaos and in a state of collapse. Hitler and the Nazi party exploited this condition to blame the Jews. As they conquered Europe they set about the systematic destruction of the Jewish race. Trains transported millions to death camps where they were gassed and their bodies burned.

That a civilised nation such as Germany, the birthplace of many great artists and the beauty they created, could commit such a crime against the whole human race is hard to grasp.

By the end of the Second World War, Germany had displaced over 26,000,000 people, many to die in concentration camps. In the main extermination camps at Auschwitz, Majdanek and Treblinka in Poland, and Buchenwald in Germany, many millions of innocent people, whose only crime was to be different, were killed by starvation, cold, disease, torture, medical experimentation and for pure sadistic pleasure.

War in the air

Battle of Britain, 1940.
Paul Nash (1889–1946).
Oil on canvas, 121.9 × 182.9 cm.
Imperial War Museum, London.

These two pictures were commissioned for the nation by the War Artists' Advisory Committee, a group set up to ensure a record of Britain at war. Even in the recent conflict in the Falkland Islands an official War Artist was present.

Project work

The First World War was a war of humans matched against the power of the machine. In the Second World War, it was more a case of machine pitted against machine. The reactions of the War Artists from the two wars reflect this. In any future conflict, machines may direct machines and people become irrelevant, except as victims.

Produce an extended set of work to reflect the effect of bombing on its victims. You might discuss the morality of inflicting such suffering.

136

Battle of Germany, 1944.
Paul Nash (1889–1946).
Oil on canvas, 121.9 × 182.9 cm.
Imperial War Museum, London.

These two paintings demonstrate the mechanised progress of the war: from the debris of German bombers broken up over Britain in 1940, to the impersonal deluge unleashed on Germany in 1944/5. The paintings, the 'Battle of Germany' a sequel to the 'Battle of Britain', embody a similar imaginative interpretation of the elements involved, though Paul Nash was very careful to base his work in each on official, factual sources.

The hit and miss of the early bombing raids had, by the end of the war, been replaced by an almost production-line efficiency. The bombing of the city of Dresden in 1945 illustrates this. Master bombers drifted high above the city, directing first one group, then another, of target markers. Each line of markers corrected those previously laid until the master bombers were certain of the target. Then, the bomber stream began its run up to the target. Up to 1,000 aircraft dropped 3,000 tons of high explosives on the city below, packed with refugees. The aircraft destroyed almost half of the city in one night. Cities like Berlin absorbed 49,000 tons of bombs in twenty-four raids. The suffering of the victims is impossible to imagine. Only nuclear weapons can wreak destruction more devastating.

Beneath the moon and a pall of rising smoke, the city waits; Nash catches the impersonal nature of the orchestrated destruction that came night after night to the homes and factories of Germany.

The Imperial War Museum in London has an unrivalled collection of the work of British War Artists. The wars fought by Britain during this century are an important part of our past; it is important that we understand them if we are to avoid them in the future.

Holiday

Laura Knight (1877–1970) painted this comfortable evocation of the pleasures of the open air. The two pictures are so different, yet have so much in common. Both are carefully constructed, thoughtful and accomplished. Both are very much in tune with the spirit of their age; they illustrate how our vision of the world has changed. Which do you prefer? Can you say why?

The Beach, 1908.
Laura Knight (1877–1970).
Oil on canvas, 127.6 × 153 cm.
Laing Art Gallery, Newcastle.

Here is a view that many tourists to the hot Mediterranean beaches are familiar with: acres of beach, covered with burning, unhealthy flesh; a twisted confusion of human figures. There seems no obvious compositional framework, but in fact there is. This is a carefully constructed picture. Can you discover the compositional structure of this painting?

Grilled in the hot sun on an Italian beach, Renato Guttuso's figures are painted in a style known as Social Realism. Guttuso is an Italian Socialist painter. Social Realism is a style of painting popular with the establishments of many Socialist and Communist countries. Where Guttuso's work differs from the official art of these countries is in a savage realism rather than an emphasis on propaganda. He cannot be accused of seeking pretty subjects: he sees his people 'warts and all'.

Beach, 1955.
Renato Guttuso (1912–1987).
Oil on canvas.
Galleria Nazionale, Parma, Italy.

Ugliness

Student's work.

It seems to have been commonly thought by the Christians of the Renaissance that beauty and holiness went closely together and that sinners were physically ugly. The religious paintings of the Renaissance are full of handsome and beautiful saints and ugly, wretched sinners.

Project work

Choose a good friend; he or she will have to be a good friend to survive this treatment!

Produce an extended set of work, based on appropriate research, including portraits drawn from life. In your drawings, change the face of your friend and make it ugly – really ugly.

Five Grotesque Heads.
Leonardo da Vinci (1452–1519).
Royal Library, Windsor.

Grotesque Heads.
Leonardo da Vinci (1452–1519).
Library of the Duke of Devonshire, Chatsworth.

Michelangelo Buonarroti explained the youth and beauty of his Virgin Mary in the Pieta sculpture in St Peter's, Rome, as due to her never having had a single sinful thought. The sinners who strike at Christ with sticks and knotted ropes in the 'Passion' by Peter Bruegel the Elder (c.1525/30–1569) are in sharp contrast to her beauty.

Leonardo da Vinci had an almost inexhaustible curiosity, and the compulsion to record all that he saw. His notebooks, of which there were thirteen containing thousands of drawings, record his methodical and scientific approach to the visual world. Leonardo saw this as a world which contained not only the fine and the beautiful but also the grotesque and the ugly. He often drew characters he saw on the streets. The grotesque portraits on this page have been chosen from the many in his notebooks.

A fruitful source for you to find 'grotesques' might be in the gargoyles of a local church. In the Middle Ages, masons liked to show off their skills by carving faces and waterspouts along the eaves of the churches they built. Very occasionally you might be lucky and find that one of them has left a self-portrait gazing down from among the devils.

Poverty

Two Peasant Boys and a Negro Boy.
Bartolomé Esteban Murillo (1618–1682).
Dulwich College Picture Gallery.

Project work

The romantic poverty of the boys as portrayed by Murillo and the calmly resigned poor of Puvis de Chavannes bear little relationship to the absolute crushing poverty seen on our television screens.

Produce an extended set of work designed to make people more aware of poverty in this country or overseas.

Shelter for the poor and the homeless is often newspapers and perhaps a cardboard box. Crumpled paper can be stuffed into the legs or sleeves of clothing to act as an insulator. A thick cardboard box is a prized possession, keeping out at least the worst of the cold and wet. Poverty is sometimes made worse by drink, often the only thing that will keep the destitute warm on long winter nights.

We know these people by the expression 'down-and-outs': an expression borrowed from boxing, where to be 'down and out' is to be knocked out, unable to rise again. They are the poorest and, despite the efforts of many kind people, the least considered of our society.

The Poor Fisherman, 1881.
Pierre Puvis de Chavannes (1824–1898).
Oil on canvas, 155 × 192 cm.
The Louvre, Paris.

Many millions of people live a life of abject poverty – they have nothing. When we see television appeals with people starving to death we react and raise money to help. In many parts of the world people live out their whole lives only marginally above this level of starvation.

What we consider to be poverty in our country would seem a life of wealth to people in some areas of the world, though this is hardly much consolation to our homeless and hopeless poor.

Gustave Doré (1832–1883) completed a set of engravings of London in Victorian times. They were published in 1871 in a book entitled *London*. It has been reprinted many times and is held by many to be his best work. See if you can obtain a copy. It shows how the poor in the last century lived in the slums of our cities. Collect newspaper cuttings, photographs and information about our urban poor. What has changed?

If you want to find out more about poverty in this country, try an experiment: make a list of all the things you consider essential to your life – shelter, food, clothing, etc. Include in your list the cost of each item; for example, find out about the cost of accommodation in your area. Find out what the official poverty line is in this country for a single person. See which of your essentials you can afford to buy. The length of the list you cannot afford is the measure of your poverty.

Old age

Mrs Mounter at the Breakfast Table, 1916.
Harold Gilman (1876–1919).
Oil on canvas, 61 × 40.6 cm.
Tate Gallery, London.

Project work

Talk to old people that you know, grandparents, friends or neighbours, and find out what they think of the modern world. Try to put yourself in their place.

Produce an extended set of work, supported by appropriate research, to explain their view of the world, the things they like, the things that worry or scare them.

To help you with your work, perhaps an old person will act as your model. Primitive tribes often venerate their elders, treating them with respect as the head of the household. Respecting the experience of old age is in everyone's interest.

Because of our technical skills and our wealth, we consider ourselves an advanced and a civilised country. Perhaps by the measure of the way we treat our old and our poor we should be less sure of our superiority.

An Old Man and His Grandson, *c.* 1480.
Domenico Ghirlandaio (1449–1494).
Tempera on a wood panel, 63 × 46 cm.
Louvre, Paris.

Make a survey of the way old people you know spend their spare time. After retirement they should have plenty of time, but have they?

On page 99 there is a drawing of a dead baby, painted as a remembrance. This charming picture of an old man and his grandson has a similar, unsuspected story. There is a drawing, on which this picture is based, that shows that the old man was in fact dead when he was drawn. The skill of the artist has transformed his dead features, has breathed love and affection again into his face.

Collect pictures of old people; record how age changes the shape of the face. Study the way the face folds and creases with age.

Murals

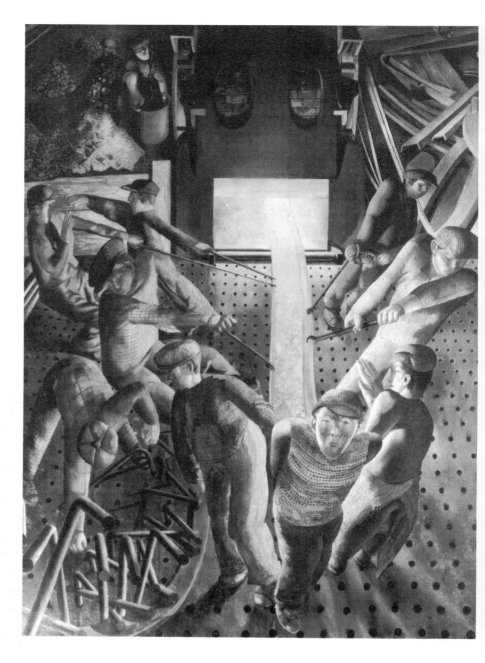

**Shipbuilding on the Clyde:
Furnaces**, 1946.
Stanley Spencer (1891–1959).
Oil on canvas, 154 × 113 cm.
Imperial War Museum, London.

Shipbuilding on the Clyde: Riveters, 1941.
Stanley Spencer (1891–1959).
Oil on canvas, 76.2 × 579.2 cm.
Imperial War Museum, London.

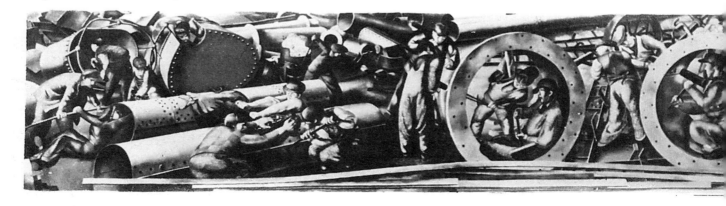

Stanley Spencer produced two great cycles of public art. Both are less well-known than they deserve; figurative painting seeming to be unfashionable in an increasingly abstract world of art. Yet to disregard them is to ignore an important part of our creative history.

The Berkshire village of Burghclere, so near to his beloved Cookham, holds the first of these murals. Spencer drew on his experiences in Macedonia in the First World War to decorate the walls of a commemorative chapel. He fills the walls of the small chapel with an amazing personal record of the war. Painted on canvas stuck to the walls, soldiers from Spencer's medical unit make beds for the wounded, clean the tea urns, butter bread, and perform any one of a number of menial tasks. Spencer used his observational skills, his eye for detail and for the unusual, to make a remarkable record of the soldiers' life. Spencer was a religious man who truly believed that man found favour with God in doing the most menial tasks in the service of his fellow man. This series of pictures is a celebration of this.

In the Second World War Spencer, together with many artists of the day, was given a commission by the War Artists' Advisory Committee. His task was to record the work of shipbuilders on the Clyde. At Port Glasgow he found a second home, a community as close-knit as his own village, and into which he was welcomed. Spencer produced a series of paintings of the shipbuilders at work. He was fascinated by the work they did. His powers of observation allowed full rein, he revelled in the strange contorted figures and the dramatic lighting.

Project work

Make a study of the practical problems of large-scale paintings. Spencer's works are, as we have seen, painted on canvas glued to the walls: effective, but prone to problems in the long term, rather as wallpaper is. Find out about the use of a cartoon in transferring a design to a wall.

Design and produce a painting on as large a scale as is possible. There are many problems and rewards associated with on this scale work. Double-thickness corrugated card can be bought in sheets 2.5 × 1.8 metres, and can be cut and joined to any practical wall size.

The figure

The Fifer.
Edouard Manet (1832–1883).
Oil on canvas, 164 × 97 cm.
Musée d'Orsay, Paris.

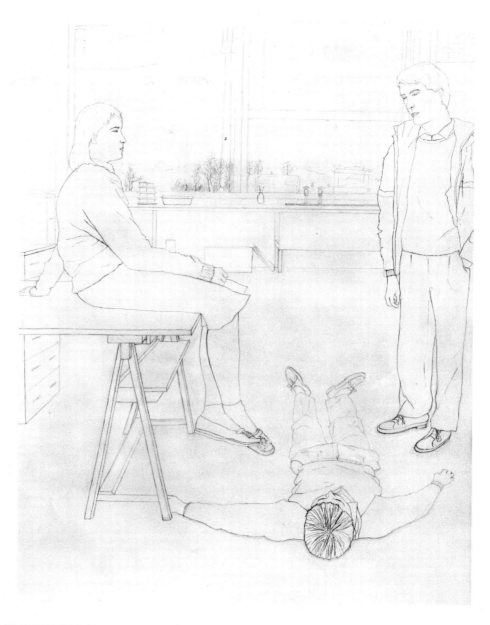

Student's work

Project work

Make a series of individual figure studies; they can be elaborate drawings or simple line drawings. In the example above, the thickness and weight of the lines is virtually the only indication of space. Combine your studies into a piece of work based on a group of figures.

The advent of abstraction destroyed the pride of place enjoyed by the human figure in works of art. Until the late 1950s, life drawing was a central activity in art colleges; since then in many cases it has become optional (although it now seems to be enjoying a return to favour in some colleges). It had become regarded as academic and without value. You only have to examine the work of those artists who continued to work with figures to realise that it was not.

149

Assessment

Students who follow an art and design course should develop a critical faculty and the vocabulary that goes with it. They should do this by analysing their own work and that of others. They will only do this if they are encouraged to discuss their work openly. They should become used to explaining to each other and to the teacher what they are doing. Only by a free discussion of ideas will they learn to do this.

The teacher's role in this is twofold. Firstly to encourage and guide discussion; secondly to make sure that assessments are talked about at length with each student. All this takes time, but I am convinced it is time well spent. There is no purpose in marking work without discussion or explanation, for to have real value, assessment should act as a guide to further progress.

Every student should have the opportunity to assess his or her own efforts and to record in some way his or her reaction to the teacher's assessment so that each time a set of work is marked the likelihood of positive improvement is strengthened. Work merely marked with a simple grade represents a valuable opportunity missed, and can give rise to resentment.

In my experience, student assessment has been most successful when the discussion is linked to preceding work. In addition to giving students a useful standard for comparison, this helps them to realise that they are involved in a continuing process; that each piece is not only related to its predecessor, but is also in some ways the basis for the next effort.

Opposite is a simple pro-forma which I have used for many years. Most students have been happy to use it and have freely filled in the comments section. As a rule students tend to be very critical of themselves and take the assessment process very seriously.

This form should not be seen as a substitute for general discussion about work in progress. The teacher's comments should be precise and specific to a set of work. The student keeps the assessment form with the work it refers to. The grade agreed can be separately kept for the purpose of records. When any re-assessment occurs the original sheet will be with the work – stuck to the reverse!

The sheer quantity of assessment now required means that, in all but the smallest groups, a formal assessment structure is necessary. An exhibition of work, though time consuming and requiring space, is a most effective way of assessing work. The advantages for all students of presenting work in a clear form and in seeing the efforts of others is not to be underestimated.

Assessment

Self assessment – tick the box *you* feel answers the question best. If you want to make any further comment use the space at the bottom of the sheet.

Is this your best work?	☐	yes	☐ no	☐	?
Have you understood the topic?	☐	yes	☐ no	☐	?
Has your work improved during the topic?	☐	yes	☐ no	☐	?
Did you complete the homework?	☐	yes	☐ no	☐	?
Could you have done better?	☐	yes	☐ no	☐	?
Are you happy with the way your work has been presented?	☐	yes	☐ no	☐	?

This is your teacher's final grade for this set of work.

Teacher's comments: _____

_____

_____

_____

Teacher's final grade

Do you agree with it? If NO say why.   ☐ yes   ☐ no   ☐ ?

Comments: _____

_____

_____

_____

_____

The artists

Learning about artists and their work can be interesting, but often it is not made as easy as it could be. Reference books sometimes use art terms to explain art terms! Keep at it though and, like a jig-saw puzzle, the pieces will eventually fit together and you will be able to put artists and their work into a context.

The artists that have been referred to in this book are listed on this page and on page 153. The name of the artist and the dates of birth and death are followed by the medium in which the artist worked and the page number(s) where his or her work is shown. The page numbers are listed in **bold**.

Ayrton, Michael (1921–1975)
British painter, sculptor, book illustrator and maze-builder: **29**

Bacon, Francis (b. 1909)
British painter: **25**

Bewick, Thomas (1753–1828)
British wood and copper engraver: **26, 27**

Blake, Peter (b. 1932)
British artist: **36**

Boucher, Francois (1703–1770)
French painter: **79**

Boyle, Mark (b. 1935)
British multi-media/multi-sensory artist: **39**

Braque, Georges (1882–1963)
French painter: **31**

Burra, Edward (1905–1976)
British painter: **59, 83**

Burri, Alberto (b. 1915)
Italian painter: **72**

Bury, Pol (b. 1922)
Belgian kinetic sculptor: **53**

Butler, Reg (1913–1981)
British sculptor: **46**

Canaletto, Antonio (1697–1768)
Venetian painter: **9, 11**

Carmago, Sergio (b. 1930)
Brazilian sculptor: **74**

Caro, Anthony (b. 1924)
British sculptor: **44**

Cassatt, Mary (1845–1926)
American painter and printmaker: **91**

Cézanne, Paul (1839–1906)
French painter: **100, 101**

Constable, John (1776–1837)
British painter: **17**

Cooper, Samuel (1608–1672)
English miniature painter: **99**

David, Jacques-Louis (1748–1825)
French painter: **107**

Degas, Edgar (1834–1917)
French painter and sculptor: **102, 103**

Dürer, Albrecht (1471–1528)
German painter and printmaker: **16, 76**

Egg, Augustus Leopold (1816–1863)
British painter: **120**

Egley, William Maw (1826–1916)
British painter: **121**

Escher, Maurits Cornelius (1898–1972)
Dutch graphic artist: **12**

Francesca, della Piero (1420–1492)
Italian painter: **8**

Friedrich, Caspar David (1774–1840)
German painter: **97**

Géricault, Théodore (1791–1824)
French painter: **94, 95, 106**

Ghirlandaio, Domenico (1449–1494)
Florentine painter: **145**

Giacometti, Alberto (1901–1966)
Swiss sculptor: **50**

Gilman, Harold (1876–1919)
British painter: **144**

Gogh, Vincent van (1853–1890)
Dutch painter: **88, 89**

Gore, Spencer (1878–1914)
British painter: **62, 63**

Greaves, Walter (1846–1931)
British painter: **77**

Grueze, Jean-Baptiste (1725–1805)
French painter: **78**

Guttoso, Renato (1912–1987)
Italian painter: **139**

Hanson, Duane (b. 1925)
American sculptor: **93**

Hilliard, Nicholas (1547–1619)
English miniature painter: **117**

Hitchens, Ivon (1893–1979)
British painter: **108**

Holbein, Hans the Younger (1497–1543)
German portrait painter: **92**

Hondius, Abraham (1625/30–1691)
Dutch painter: **23**

Hunt, Alfred William (1830–1896)
British painter: **58**

Hunt, William Holman (1827–1910)
British painter: **134**

Network

The references on these two pages show how the subject can be supported by other sources. It is not exhaustive.

From an early date artists travelled and, in their sketch-books, kept records of what they saw on their journeys. Many travelled to Italy to see the wonders of Ancient Rome and the Renaissance. Albrecht Dürer (1471–1528) made an outstanding series of landscape drawings and watercolours of his journeys across the Alps and into Italy.

John Constable (1776–1837) recorded the landscape of Suffolk. He believed in studying direct from nature. This gave us such work as the 'Cloud Studies' (1816–1822) of which several are in the Victoria and Albert Museum. The knowledge and experience he gained from such studies can be seen in 'The Haywain' (1821) in the National Gallery, London. The idea of painting direct from nature influenced the *plein air* painters in nineteenth-century France.

Also at work in rural East Anglia was the Norwich School. John Crome (1768–1821) was the painter who established this 'school' of artists who exhibited together. A good example of Crome's work is the 'Poringland Oak' painted in 1818 and now in the Tate Gallery, London.

An example of the watercolour work for which this 'school' is now known is 'Greta Bridge' by John Sell Cotman (1782–1842) in the British Museum, London.

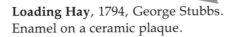

Loading Hay, 1794, George Stubbs. Enamel on a ceramic plaque.

J. M. W. Turner (1775–1851) gained his fame and reputation as a painter of topographical landscapes. 'Buttermere Lake, with a part of Crummack Water, Cumberland: a shower' (1797) in the Tate Gallery, London, is a good example of this facet of his work. See also his painting 'The Falls of Clyde' (page 80) in the Walker Art Gallery, Liverpool. There is a wide selection of this type of his work available for study.

Thomas Girtin (1775–1802) worked with Turner on many occasions. 'Kirkstall Abbey, Evening (c.1800) in the Victoria and Albert Museum is a good example of his work. Just before he died, Girtin visited Paris to draw views.

John Robert Cozen's (1752–1797) watercolour painting of Padua (1782) shows that artists (he was English) were prepared to go a long way for their subjects. It is in the Tate Gallery, London.

William Wordsworth's (1770–1850) love of nature can be seen in his nature poems. His sister Dorothy catalogued their journeys through the beautiful Lake District. Moonlit walks and long journeys over the fells are reflected in his poetry.

The poetry of John Clare (1793–1864), whose simple direct verses record the love of wild creatures and places, underlies our feeling for landscape.

The early landscapes were views of or from the country houses of the rich.

Jan Siberecht's (c.1627–c.1700) 'Landscape with Rainbow, Henley on Thames' (1695) in the Tate Gallery, London, is an example of an early topographical landscape. Early maps, with their decorative borders and crests, are a useful source for study. The paintings of Antonio Canaletto (1697–1768) at Warwick Castle and Albury Park are good examples of an interest in ancient monuments. Richard Wilson (1713–1782) with his painting of 'Pembroke Town and Castle' (c.1773) in the National Museum of Wales, is a good example of 'home-grown' talent.

John Everett Millais' (1829–1896) 'The Blind Girl (1856) in the Birmingham City Art Gallery or William Holman Hunt's (1827–1910) 'Strayed Sheep' (1852) show a landscape of an imaginary golden age.

The Pre-Raphaelite group created an idealised form of landscape. There are many good examples, either in their own right or as backgrounds to morality pictures. The work of Ivon Hitchens (1873–1979) takes landscape apart and uses its elements as the basis for broad studies in colour. For painters of the de-populated rural landscapes of the twentieth century, try John Nash (1873–1977) whose 'Park Scene, Great Glenham' (1943) in the Walker Art Gallery, Liverpool, is a good example of his work. Another example is 'The Cornfield' (1918) in the Tate Gallery, London. Thomas Hardy (1840–1928) wrote descriptions of the West Country in his novels. *The Woodlanders* (1886–87) is a good example.

Land Art uses creatively the materials found in the landscape. Earth, stone, wood and other natural materials are assembled within the Art Gallery or in a natural setting. On a larger scale, tons of material can be moved out-of-doors to create works like, 'Spiral Jetty' (1970) by Robert Smithson (1938–1973).

Richard Long (b. 1945) records his journeys through the landscape by photography, by writing down key experiences or observations, and by maps. This can be seen in '100 Mile Walk' in the Tate Gallery, London.

Aerial or satellite photographs, weather maps or the coloured pictures taken from the air by infra-red sensors, can all be useful sources of ideas.

Landscape

Capability Brown (1716–1783) looked for the 'capabilities' (i.e. possibilities) in landscape; the way that landscape could be altered to achieve a sense of harmony and peace. To that end he dug lakes, moved rivers and planted trees and whole forests. The beautiful settings of many of our country houses were designed by Brown and his followers.

Some country houses have views transformed to match paintings. Pictures by Salvator Rosa (1615–1673) were favourites for these dramatic landscapes. Corsham Court in Wiltshire has some fine examples of this type of view painting.

Network

The references on these two pages show how the subject can be supported by other sources.

L. S. Lowry (1887–1976) recorded the industrial life of our cities: the crowded streets, the workers rushing from the factory gates or waiting for the commuter train. His work is worth the extra study required to lose the 'matchstick men' image!

Look at Constantin Meunier's (1831–1905) 'The Puddler', bronze, which is in the Brussels Museum, Belgium. 'The Puddler' works in a steel mill; he stirs the molten steel to prevent a crust forming. With his hands and face close to the liquid metal, it is exhausting and hot work. His greatest piece, the culmination of all his work to glorify the labour of the working class, is his 'Monument to Labour' (1901), Place de Trooz, Brussels.

The Artists' International Association, founded in 1933, was an avowed socialist group whose membership and work reflected this standpoint.

Clive Branson's (1907–1944) picture 'Selling the Daily Worker outside the Projectile Engineering Works' (1937) which is in a private collection, or Percy Hortons (1897–1970) 'Unemployed Man' (1936) in the Sheffield City Art Gallery, are examples of their work.

Emile Zola (1840–1902) wrote his novel *Germinal* to describe the grim struggle between the miners and their employers in Northern France.

Trade union flags and banners are a fruitful source of images from our own past and present.

Robert Tressel wrote *The Ragged Trousered Philanthropists* about the life of painters and decorators in Hastings.

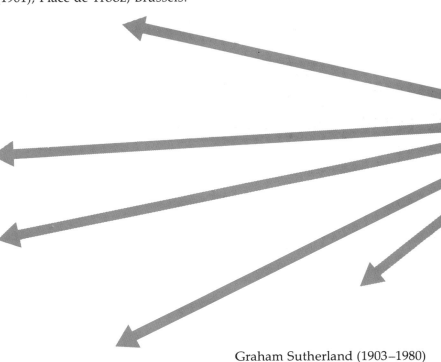

A dramatic view of the industrial landscape by Philippe Jacques de Loutherbourg can be seen on page 130. 'Coalbrookdale by Night (1801) is in the Science Museum, London. Stanley Spencer's (1891–1959) shipyard workers form his work for the War Artists' Advisory Committee can be found in the Imperial War Museum. Examples can be found on page 146 and page 147.

Graham Sutherland (1903–1980) portrayed conditions in the Cornish tin mines as in 'Tin Mine: Emerging Miner' (1944) in the Leeds City Art Gallery.

'Ruby Loftus screwing the breech ring in a Bofors Gun' (1942) by Dame Laura Knight (1877–1970) in the Imperial War Museum, London, is a good example of women's contribution to war work.

A new experience is a good time for an artist to begin to make a record. Unfamiliar sights, sounds and sensations are best recorded when they are fresh, before familiarity dulls the senses. Many students have paper rounds, Saturday work or evening jobs and most take part in work experience programmes. Make a record of your own experience of work.

Numerous folk songs and ballads describe the sailor's life. Clarkson Stanfield (1793–1867), a sailor himself, painted 'Off the Dogger Bank' in 1846. It is in the Victoria and Albert Museum, London. The most famous recorder of the sailor's life, and of ships and the moods of the sea, is the painter, J. M. W. Turner (1775–1851). There is an extensive body of his work reflecting his intense interest in the sea.

Tobias Smolett (1721–1771) wrote in his novel, *The adventures of Roderick Random*, of the sailor's life.

The French painters of peasant life like Jean-Francois Millet (1814–1875) and Camille Pissarro (1830–1903) show rural life at its starkest. Their work, supported by numerous drawings, are a powerful statement of the reality of manual labour in the countryside. There are good examples of Millet's work in the National Gallery, London ('The Winnower at Work') and in the National Museum of Wales ('The Peasant Family'). This tradition is carried on in the drawings of Georges Seurat (1859–1891), for example, 'The Gleaner' on page 113.

Emile Zola wrote the novel *La Terre* (The Earth) to describe the life of the French peasant.

Work

In contrast, the workers of rural England are often portrayed in an idealised form, as in William Holman Hunt's 'Hireling Shepherd'.
Thomas Hardy (1840–1928) wrote of a similarly romanticised countryside in his novel *Tess of the D'Urbervilles*.

Sir George Clausen (1852–1944) comes close to the realism of Millet's work in an English context. His work, however, harks back to an age that had passed away by the time he painted it – even in 1900 the land was farmed by machines (horse or steam-powered) and manual labour was an outdated way of working the land. Look at 'The Boy and the Man' (1900) in the Bradford Art Galleries and Museums.

Look for examples of the industrial pottery and the work of Josiah Wedgewood (1730–1795). Wedgewood was a friend and patron of Joseph Wright (1734–1797) of Derby whose paintings of early industrial landscapes and people at work are some of the few pictures of this period of our industrial history. 'The Iron Forge' by Joseph Wright, in the Broadlands Collection, Hampshire, is typical of this strand in his work. Though recording the working life of a later period in the potteries area of Staffordshire, the novels of Arnold Bennett provide vivid background material. *Clayhanger* is a good example.

George Stubbs (1724–1806) painted some fine scenes of work in the countryside. 'The Reapers' and 'Haymakers' in the Tate Gallery, London, are two good examples of this type of work.

Another author who provides background reading for people at work in industrial Britain is Charles Dickens (1812–1870), for example, *Hard Times*.

Glossary

Acrylic paint A tough, flexible paint that retains its brilliance. It is a synthetic paint often thinned with water, though waterproof when dried.

Anamorphosis A distorted image which only appears normal from a particular viewpoint or in a curved mirror or lens.

Aquatint A printmaking technique, often associated with etching. A metal plate (usually of copper or zinc) is sprinkled with powdered resin. When the plate is heated, the resin is fixed in place in the form of tiny melted globules. The plate is then placed in a bath of acid, which eats out the un-protected areas between the melted resin globules. The longer the plate remains in the acid, the deeper the bite; and the deeper the bite, the stronger the eventual print. A variety of tones may therefore be created by removing the plate from the acid from time to time and 'stopping out' selected areas with an acid-resistant varnish. Where the sprinkling of resin is very fine, the printed effect is rather like washes of watercolour; coarser sprinklings produce a rich speckled texture.

Assemblage A three-dimensional piece of work containing manufactured or natural materials not usually associated with sculpture.

Black-lead See metalpoint.

Block A flat-surfaced piece of material (usually wood or linoleum) in which a design is cut and from which a print may be made.

Bronze A sculpture material, usually cast. Bronze is an alloy, mainly of copper but with a high proportion of tin. It is durable, has strength, yet will hold fine detail and subtle textures.

Camera obscura This literally means 'dark room', which is exactly what the early forms of camera were. The camera obscura was invented in the 16th century as a means of making accurate drawings of views. Light enters a darkened room, tent, or large box and, by means of an arrangement of lenses and mirrors, an image of the view outside is projected onto a surface. It is then an easy matter for the artist to trace it. Such devices exist at Oxford and at Dundee.

Cartoon Today, the word usually refers to a humorous drawing. Originally, however, it meant a full-size preparatory drawing for a large wall or ceiling painting. The word comes from the Italian *cartone*, meaning a large piece of paper.

Charcoal A drawing material formed by charring willow under intense heat.

Collage The word comes from the French, and means something glued or pasted. A collage is an image created by means of sticking material (usually torn or cut paper) to the picture surface.

Drypoint A print produced by scratching an image into the surface of a metal plate with a sharp steel point. The steel point ploughs a furrow in the plate, and the displaced metal raises a 'burr' along-side the furrow. The plate is covered with stiff ink, which is then wiped away with muslin. The raised 'burrs', however, still hold ink and print as soft, velvety lines.

Engraving Cutting grooves into a plate of metal or a block of wood to create a surface from which a print may be made. Prints made in this way are referred to as engravings.

Fibreglass See glass fibre.

Glass fibre A resin plastic strengthed by strands, tape or rope of finely extruded glass.

Graphite A natural form of carbon, which, when mixed with china clay, produces pencil 'lead'.

Kinetic sculpture Sculpture designed to move or having moving parts.

Linocut A print made from an image cut into lino-leum. This is quite a modern technique, derived from wood-block cutting. Linoleum (or lino) is much softer and easier to cut than wood, however, and can be made even more soft by gentle warm-ing.

Lithography A printing method which relies on the fact that water runs off a greasy surface, and that greasy substances will not 'take' on a wet surface. A drawing is made with greasy ink or a greasy crayon on absorbent limestone or on specially prepared zinc. The stone or zinc is then wetted, and a greasy ink is applied to the surface with a roller. The ink will only adhere to the drawn marks. The print, which is made by transferring the image to paper in a special press, is called a lithograph.

Maquette A small sculpture made as a trial for a larger piece.

Medium (plural **media**) The technical methods employed by an artist or the tools and materials associated with those methods.

Metalpoint A fine drawing point which may be of gold, lead or copper. Results are often much finer and more delicate than pencil drawings.

Monoprint A print taken from an inked, painted, or dyed surface. Because no cutting is involved, and the printing is simply a matter of pressing paper onto inked, painted, or dyed marks, the image is not exactly repeatable.

Motif A unit of a repeat pattern or design. The word is also sometimes used to refer to an artist's subject – usually a landscape.

Perspective A systematic way of representing a three-dimensional form on a flat surface.

Photomontage A technique of creating an original piece of work from cut and re-assembled pictures, photographs, etc. A seamless image may be created by photocopying the original.

Quill A drawing or writing pen formed from the flight feathers of a goose or swan. The pen is cut across its wide end either at an angle or to form a square tip. The hollow shaft forms a natural ink reservoir.

Reed pen A pen cut from a reed or cane. It is less flexible than a quill.

Resin A transparent solid substance derived from the hardened sap of certain trees. There are now many synthetic substitutes.

Scale The dimensions and proportions of an image or object.

Scraperboard A sheet of card covered with fine china clay and then a thin layer of, usually, black ink. Images are created by scratching through with a sharp tool to reveal the white clay below.

Screenprint A method of printing by which ink is forced with a squeegee (a rubber or plastic blade) through a fine mesh onto a sheet of paper or board. Areas of the mesh can be blocked out to prevent the ink going through. The design or image is created by selectively blocking out different areas of the screen.

Silverpoint See metalpoint.

Tempera A paint with gum as a binder, to hold the paint together when dry.

Wood-engraving A print produced by engraving into the polished end-grain surface of a block of boxwood. Since the wood is so hard, and there is no direction to the grain, the wood will accept extremely fine detail and may freely be engraved in any direction.